Cowboy Fiddler

Titles of Related Interest

Horse Fixin': Forty Years of Working with Problem Horses
by Frankie McWhorter as told to John R. Erickson

Play it Lazy: The Bob Wills Fiddle Legacy
by Lanny Fiel and Frankie McWhorter, with an audiocassette by
Frankie McWhorter produced by John R. Erickson

Cowboy Fiddler

By Frankie McWhorter

As Told to John R. Erickson

Foreword by William W. Savage, Jr.

Afterword by Charles R. Townsend

TEXAS TECH UNIVERSITY PRESS

Acknowledgment

I would like to thank John Erickson for jeopardizing his health and his marriage to write this book.

This book was set in 10 on 13 ITC Bookman and printed on acid-free paper that meets the guidelines for permanence and durability of the Committee on Production Guidelines for Book Longevity of the Council on Library Resources. ∞

Cover art by Tom Floyd
Jacket and book design by Kelley Ferguson Farwell

Manufactured in the United States of America

Library of Congress Cataloging-in-Publication Data
McWhorter, Frankie.
    Cowboy fiddler / by Frankie McWhorter and John R. Erickson ; foreword by William W. Savage, Jr. ; afterword by Charles R. Townsend.
        p. cm.
    ISBN 0-89672-248-1.
    1. McWhorter, Frankie. 2. Cowboys—Texas—Biography.
3. Fiddlers—Texas—Biography. 4. Texas—Social life and customs.
5. Texas—Biography. I. Erickson, John R., 1943- . II. Title.
F391.4.M28A3 1991
976.4′063′092—dc20
[B]   91-16244
                                                  CIP

Texas Tech University Press
Lubbock, Texas 79409-1037 USA

92 93 94 95 96 97 98 99 / 9 8 7 6 5 4 3 2

Contents

In Memory of Boyd Rogers

Foreword

Cowboy memoir has been a staple of Western Americana since 1885 when Charles A. Siringo published *A Texas Cow-Boy; or, Fifteen Years on the Hurricane Deck of a Spanish Pony.* At the time, Siringo held the more prosaic job of serving customers in a Caldwell, Kansas, ice cream parlor. He had turned to writing as an easier way to make some money, embracing memoir as his métier only after fiction proved too difficult for him to manage. Over the next forty years, Siringo published essentially the same story several times more, which suggested to many other cowboys and former cowboys the earning power of experience. Library shelves nowadays groan and sag beneath the accumulated weight of cowboy memoir, an indication that publishers—including a fair number of university presses—have found the stuff lucrative as well. So plentiful has it been in this century that, sometime in the next one, quantifiers may come to describe cowboy reminiscence in terms of gross tonnage and include it along with beef, oil, and ore in measurements of the West's productivity. But the cynical reader who pauses here to ask, "Well, if that's so, why do we need more of it?" should contemplate mankind's eternal search for a better mousetrap. While we have cowboy memoir aplenty, we do not have a whole lot that is very good or very useful. In *Cowboy Fiddler* we have something that most assuredly is both.

Imagerial cowboys occupy our attention in novels or films because we know they have been places, seen sights, and done things; and as we read or watch, our assumption is that they will go, see, and do again, all for our amusement. We know from the history that real cowboys had some sense of the effect of physical mobility upon their lives. It accounted for experience, which was a thing to be had in town, in the next county, up the trail, or

vii

wherever the job took them. And experience, in large measure, became the grist of the cowboys' own campfire entertainments— the stories, the songs, the recitations that are the basis not only of cowboy lore but also of cowboy culture. Too often these days, cowboy culture (if it is meant to imply more than tending cows) is reduced (by fashion designers, journalists, and not a few scholars who ought to know better) to matters of style without indications of substance, so that the very term is taken to be a synonym for what you buy from Ralph Lauren to wear to a barbecue, instead of a label for a conscious system of values transmitted from one generation to the next through art or literature or music.

There are still real cowboys, and they still transmit culture, whether the general public happens to be aware of it. The annual "gatherings" of cowboy poets in Elko, Nevada, comprise the principal visible evidence of the process; and the occasional appearances of cowboy poets on late-night television talk shows mark the extent of its exposure. Whenever cowboy culture is to be found, it does enjoy some popularity, however; and for that reason the cowboys one meets today in public places are more likely to have calluses from fingering guitar strings than they are from pulling leather since sunup. If there is any doubt of that, the business card a cowboy presents, complete with phone numbers to call for "bookings," will offer confirmation. The public *assumes* cowboy status on the basis of a) clothes, b) demeanor, and c) the culture in transmission. But the assumption begs the question, and the cowboy one contemplates on a stage and under the lights may long since have severed occupational connections with ranch and range. The art of the poet, like the athleticism of the bronc rider, may by virtue of previous employment, qualify for coverage under the "cowboy" umbrella; but in both cases, practitioners are, like Owen Wister's Virginian, cowboys *sans* cows in a pastoral context, or at least lately. The irony is that such individuals extend the reputation of cowboy culture while at the same time jeopardizing its credibility.

With Frankie McWhorter one need harbor no such concerns. His is a memoir wherein the work informs the culture and the culture validates the work. Indeed, *Cowboy Fiddler* goes farther toward explaining the symbiosis of work and culture in the structure of American rural life than any account one is likely to find upon those aforementioned groaning shelves; and for that reason, if for no other, it deserves attention. Happily, however, there are other reasons too, including the sheer joy to be derived from reading the recollections of a man who knows a couple of things and has no need to be pretentious about it. As well, there is the participation of John R. Erickson to relish. Many an old cowboy with tales to tell would swap his best boots for a Boswell of Erickson's stature. His collaboration here with Frankie Mc-Whorter proves anew that it takes one to know one. Readers won't find a better demonstration of an efficacious literary partnership; and when it comes to explications of cowboy culture you just can't ask for more than that.

William W. Savage, Jr.

Introduction

By the summer of 1987, I had heard a lot of talk about a man named Frankie McWhorter, who managed a ranch over in Lipscomb County. I'd heard that he was a great fiddle player. I'd heard that he was a cowboy—a real cowboy. And I'd been told more than once that I ought to write a book about him.

I'm very particular about whom and what I choose as the subject for a book. Most people, even interesting people, don't have a book's worth of stories to tell. Ace Reid did, and I wrote a book about him in 1983. But Ace is an extraordinary man. You don't find his kind walking around every day.

I have known writers for whom writing a book was simply an exercise in discipline. They could pick almost any subject, do some research on it, and crank out a book. It might be a diet book today, a novel about Sam Houston tomorrow, and a book on Indian jewelry next month. I admire the people who can do that, and it's probably the mark of a professional writer, but I have never been able to operate that way. My books grow out of a passionate interest and a strong emotional involvement with the subject. You might say that I'm not free to choose my subjects; they choose me.

I didn't doubt that someone should write a book about Frankie McWhorter, but I doubted that I was the one to do it. There was only one way that I could find out: go to Lipscomb County and study Frankie at work. As the song says, "Don't call him a cowboy until you've seen him ride." There's wisdom in that sentence. The only way you'll ever know whether a man's a real cowboy or a real talker is to watch him out in the pasture. What matters is not so much what he says as what he does and how he does it. You have to wait and watch.

So one day in June, I called him up and asked if he could stand some company the next day. He said, "Sure! Come on over and bring your saddle. I need to ride through some cattle and we'll show you some country. And bring that banjo. I want to hear you play that thing."

I arrived at the Gray Ranch around 8:30 the next morning. In the circle drive in front of the white frame house, there was a red three-quarter–ton Ford pickup with an eighteen-foot gooseneck trailer hooked on behind. This was a flatbed pickup with a feed box behind the cab. Behind the feed box lay the spare tire, and sitting on the spare was a red roan cowdog. This must be Hank. Frankie had told me that he owned a Hank. Swallows darted through the air, catching insects and returning to their mud nests in the barn. Two horses stood in the corrals with a goat nearby.

Frankie had a pot of coffee waiting. He poured us both a cup and we sat at the dining bar in his kitchen. For an hour or more, we talked about grass, cattle, horses, cowboying, ranches for sale, spurs, dogs—the usual topics.

Then Frankie stood up, grimacing and grumbling about a catch he'd thrown into his back the day before, and suggested that we head for the pasture before it got too hot. He pulled on his high-topped riding boots with the spurs already attached and went jingling across the kitchen floor and out onto the screen porch.

There, he said a few words to Clyde, a very peculiar-looking cat. The last half of his tail had been skinned clean, so that he resembled a cross between a cat and a possum. The skinning was the work of Hank, who came up to greet us when we stepped out the door. Hank, I gathered, didn't have much use for cats.

We went to the barn just west of the house and saddled two horses. I would be riding a paint called Flower and Frankie chose a nice-looking sorrel whose name I never heard. He was a barrel horse that someone had brought for Frankie to "fix," as he called it. The horse had great potential but also some bad habits.

Flower, he explained, had come out of Benny Beutler's string of bucking horses, which wasn't something I had wanted to hear.

Flower had given Frankie a bad time and had bucked him off once on the other side of the creek, but the horse had straightened out and was doing all right.

In the barn, I noticed Frankie hobbling toward the saddle room. I asked if he wanted me to saddle his horse. He said no, he wasn't that crippled up yet. He grumbled against the pain but managed to get his horse saddled.

We loaded the horses into his gooseneck trailer and headed south. We drove through the ranch, checking windmills and counting yearlings and talking about the condition of the country. June of 1987 had been one of the wettest on record and the grass was incredible. I had never seen better grass in the Panhandle. When we came to a big set of welded pipe shipping pens, Frankie stopped the pickup and we walked through them. His boss, Roger Gray, had told him to build a good set of pens, so Frankie had ordered a load of two-inch pipe, hired a welder, and designed the pens himself, incorporating all the features he had learned during his forty years as a cowboy. He was proud of them, as he should have been. They were a masterpiece of pen building.

From there, we drove seven miles south to Higgins and ate lunch in a cafe on the east edge of town. Just about everyone who came in spoke to Frankie and joshed with him, even the banker who was holding three of his overdrafts.

After lunch we drove to another part of the ranch, where we rode through and counted a bunch of two-year-old heifers that were running with brangus bulls.

Regardless of where we were or what we were doing, we carried on a lively conversation, usually about Frankie's favorite subject, horses. It didn't take me long to realize that he was an expert on the subject and that he had spent a lifetime studying them from every possible angle.

As we drove down country roads, he pointed to horses standing a quarter-mile away, called them by name, and told me something about them. He discussed the horses he had worked with in the past six months, and I began to understand that he had quite a reputation as a horse-fixer. People who had horses with problems took them to Frankie, which meant that he was never mounted on a finished horse, the kind of horse you and I would choose to ride.

He talked about some of the worst horses he had ever come across, a JA bronc named Twilight and another called Blaze. After telling about these two outlaws, he smiled and said, "After working on the JA, I don't worry much about the horses people bring me today. They're easy compared to those JA horses that tried to kill you every time you went to throw a saddle on them."

In the cool of evening, we prowled several more pastures and made it back to headquarters at dusk. We unsaddled the horses and Frankie fed them some grain.

"Tell you what," he said, coming out of the barn, "I have to be over at the Tubb place at six o'clock tomorrow morning to help Jimmy Fry gather some cattle. You're welcome to go with me if you want, but . . . "

"I'll go."

"Good. We'll leave old Flower up for you."

I hadn't come prepared to stay the night but I wasn't ready to leave. I had seen a lot of Frankie during the day but I knew there was more.

We went into the house and Frankie told me to get out my banjo. I did and played him some of the songs from my Hank the Cowdog series of tapes: "Buzzard Love," "Hank's Lullaby," "The Saddle Up Overture in C-Maybe," "I'm Rich," and "Daddy Packed His Suitcase 'Cause Momma Was a Mean Old Bag."

Frankie listened to the songs, chuckled, and shook his head. "Son, those are good songs! They're a little bit crazy, but they're good."

Then he took off his shirt and went for his fiddle. He sat back down and began playing. He wasn't trying to put my little musical talent into perspective, but he sure did. For two straight hours, he played one fiddle tune after another. These were different from any I had heard him do before—not western swing but old-time reels and breakdowns, many of which he had learned from Bob Wills.

He executed them with the authority of a man who had total command of his instrument and with a degree of precision that took my breath away. He played on all five strings and from one end of the neck to the other.

Where had he learned all those songs? How had he learned them when he didn't read music? How did he remember them all? How could those horse breaker's hands adjust to the critical tolerances on a violin's neck, the fractions of an inch that made a note either very right or very wrong?

Somewhere between midnight and one o'clock I realized that we hadn't eaten anything since lunch. Frankie apologized and offered to cook up something, but by then I had divined that Frankie was no chef. I suggested that we draw from his collection of canned hash, soup, and potted meat.

We each had a can of "vy-eena" sausage, as Frankie called it, with soda crackers and mustard. In the months to come, I would speak of that dish as a Frankie Casserole.

At 1:30 we called it quits and went to bed. It was a short night. Frankie's alarm went off at 4:00 and he went out to grain the horses. He let me sleep until 4:45, a small payment on the deficit we had run up the night before.

He had the coffee made when I came into the kitchen. I poured myself a cup and joined him at the dinner bar. The minutes passed. I glanced around, looking for a skillet or a package of bacon or something that would indicate a plan for breakfast. The kitchen was just as we had left it the night before.

Then he stood up and said it was time to saddle the horses, and I realized that we had just drunk our breakfast. Coffee.

We saddled the horses, loaded them in the trailer, and drove south to the Jones and Jones ranch, where we picked up a young cowboy named Ronnie Evans. We loaded his dun horse into the trailer and proceeded west and south and arrived at the Tubb place after sunrise.

We worked there until noon, then ate chicken fried steaks at a small cafe in Lipscomb. After lunch, Frankie and I checked the cattle in two more of his pastures and made it back to the house around three o'clock.

By that time, I had seen enough. I knew that Frankie was someone very special, and that I had to do a book about him.

I brought up the subject that evening over supper. (More Vienna sausage). At first he tried to argue that he wasn't worth a book, but that didn't go far. I think he knew better. Then he said that he was honored that I would consider such a thing, and that maybe we ought to give it a try.

If Frankie had only been a great cowboy, horsebreaker, or fiddle player, I would have been able to resist doing a book on him. But the sheer magnitude of his knowledge, experience, and talent made him a subject I couldn't walk away from.

Most of us do well to attain proficiency in one field, perhaps two at the most. Frankie had mastered three. Part of his secret, I think, was that he required very little sleep. He could cowboy all day and play the fiddle all night, then get up and do it again the next day. At the rate he burned energy, I calculated that his actual age was somewhere between 110 and 125 years.

He had phenomenal energy, and just being around him for a few days wore me to a frazzle. I would have to go home and sleep for several days to recover.

And he had still another talent that made him a wonderful subject for a book (it wasn't his cooking). To my delight, I found him to be an accomplished storyteller.

There may be better cowboys around than Frankie. There may be better horse breakers and horse trainers, and there may be better fiddle players, although I wouldn't want to bet my own money on it. But I would bet my own money that there is no one alive today who is better at all three, and can tell about them better, than Frankie McWhorter.

When I made the decision to do a book on Frankie, I supposed that I would gather the material and write it up in my own voice, the voice of the author or biographer. But once he began telling his stories—and they came in torrents, one right after another—I realized that I couldn't tell them as well as he could.

If I couldn't improve his stories, then I should leave him alone and let him do the talking. The voice should be his.

There are a few disadvantages to this approach. Storytellers come out of an oral tradition. They're accustomed to talking, not writing, and sometimes when you take a spoken story and freeze it on a page of type, you find that something has been lost.

A story that made perfect sense out in the pasture might seem disorganized and flat on a piece of paper. What is missing, of course, is the storyteller who "sells" his story through the use of his hands, eyes, and facial expressions.

It is surprising how much a storyteller doesn't have to say to make his story work. I have heard Frankie tell stories that were wonderful, and only later did I realize that I had no idea where or when it happened. At the time, it didn't matter. The story was more important than its context.

Stories are not the same as history, and in selecting a format for Frankie's material, I had to choose between the two. I chose to leave them as stories and to stay out of his way as much as possible. Had I tried to add context and explanations, through footnotes, italics, and editor's notes, it would have spoiled the effect of the storytelling.

My role became that of a conduit, a translator from the spoken word to the written word. There are tricks to doing that, and the ultimate trick is to make the author/editor/translator invisible. The reader should be able to read the story and believe that he is hearing it, right from the mouth of the speaker, without being conscious of the author/editor/translator lurking in the background. One result of this approach is that the stories are sometimes short on detail. I have tried to add as much information about time and place as I can, without becoming a nuisance, but there might be times when the reader wishes for more.

But remember, this book is not a biography or a history; it's a book of stories. If we don't know what Frankie was doing in a certain year, it's because he didn't consider it important enough to mention. He tells stories. He doesn't write history.

I gathered most of this material in the summer and fall of 1987, and my research methods were fairly simple. I moved into Frankie's house, lived with him for days at a time, and worked with him on the ranch. He told stories when they came to him and I recorded them on a small Lanier tape recorder that I carried in the top of my boot.

We might be driving across the ranch in his pickup, riding pastures ahorseback, eating lunch in Higgins, feeding horses in the barn, building fence, or sitting around his kitchen at two o'clock in the morning. But wherever we were, Frankie was always in his own environment, telling stories in a setting that was comfortable to him. My job then was to transcribe the stories, organize them, and polish the language so that it made a successful transition from the spoken word to the printed word.

There is no question in my mind that Frankie's stories would have been admired by the likes of J. Frank Dobie, Will James, Will Rogers, Charlie Russell, Ben K. Green, and Spike Van Cleve. I am just as sure that the integrity of his cowboy experiences would have impressed Fay Ward, whose knowledge of old-time cowboying was unsurpassed.

Some of the stories that follow tell of bad horses and wild cattle. Some modern readers will wince at his descriptions, for he doesn't bother to perfume the truth. He tells what happened and makes no apology for it. After all, in most of these incidents he was just a young man trying to stay alive.

I consider myself a lucky man to have known Frankie McWhorter, to have played music with him, worked cattle with him, watched him working with his horses, and listened to his stories. He is one of the most remarkable men I've ever met and he has brought joy into my life.

I'll say about Frankie what he often said about Bob Wills and Boyd Rogers: I'm a better man for having known him.

John R. Erickson

1

Frankie McWhorter's Favorite Horse and Cowboy Stories

A lot of people wouldn't believe that we had steers that weighed sixteen hundred to eighteen hundred pounds, but it's true, we did. And if you'd tell 'em that you used to rope and tie them down on a bronc, they wouldn't believe that either. But we did.

I never did break horses on the JA's. I wish I had. I would rather have ridden raw broncs than some of them we had to ride that had all this *knowledge.*

Cowboying on the JA Ranch

I went to work for the JA's in the spring of 1948 for ninety dollars a month. I didn't finish my senior year of high school at Memphis, Texas.

I had got in trouble for something I didn't do in school, so I just throwed my books in the principal's office and left. When the JA wagon pulled out that spring, I was with it.

They had some good cowboys out there: C. H. Long, Rex Long, Jiggs Mann, Bud Long, Jack Curry, Jack Ray, and Floyd Freeman. Floyd was Shorty Freeman's father. Boy Blackwell was the wagon boss when I went there, and Bill Word was the foreman. He was an elderly person and a whale of a cowboy.

C. H. Long was one of the best cowboys I ever knew. Maybe I say that because he took a little extra time with me. He was the range boss. Some of that old country was pretty sorry and you couldn't run as many cattle per section as you could on other country, and that was his job, to determine how many went where. He kind of set up the operation.

He was a very intelligent man. He came from Throckmorton, off the Swenson ranch. His father was a cowboy down there, and later they were both at the JA's. His father lived at headquarters and took care of the chores.

Berl Teague was from Superior, Arizona. What we thought was rough country wasn't rough to Berl. He said on Sunday they'd go try to rope those wild burros for fun, like they have steer ropings here and saddle bronc riding in Montana. They'd try to rope them burros. He said it was next to impossible to get a loop on one.

He was a dally man and he carried about a sixty-foot rope when he got to the JA's, and he spent quite a lot of time trying to get it back. Those wild cows would fork a mesquite before he could get his dally laid. Them old horses, you couldn't get one of them turned around in fifteen minutes. They weren't good for a dally man. But he could use just about all of that sixty-foot rope. I've seen him catch a loose horse almost to the end of it. He was an artist with a rope.

Our ways of doing things were as foreign to him as his ways were to us. He said that cholla cactus out in Arizona was the worst enemy of a cowboy. They had to put a leather piece over a horse's chest. He said they were always ruining a good horse on it. He never mentioned that it was hard on a man but I'm sure it was.

Tom Blasingame was a camp man when I was there. He's still out there, in his nineties,[1] and I've heard he still breaks his own horses. Tom would give his horses funny names: Slip Along, "Montiosa," which meant slick or greasy, hard to hold. I'm pretty sure Tom was the one who told me, "Don't ever let a big steer you've roped get above you. He'll sure get you. Stay on the uphill side."

I don't guess I've ever known another man who was more respected by the other cowboys. Tom was the kind of person that you cared what he thought. That was the effect he had on the men. When Tom Blasingame said something, *everybody* listened.

You know, you had to prove yourself to those old guys on the JA's. They didn't just take you at face value. You had to do something to make them respect you. Normally, you can visit with a man for two minutes and know if he's a cowboy, but still, when he goes out to do something, he's got to do the right things to impress the old men.

Talking about respect, I remember when they brought Boots O'Neil out to the wagon for the first time. He was a little bitty feller, probably about sixteen years old. They brought him an old second- or third-year bronc. It wasn't the pitchingest thing on the place, but he could sure 'nuff buck. All of them could buck pretty hard.

[1.] Thomas Everett Blasingame died December 27, 1989.

It took a couple of us to ear the horse down and get Boots on him, and I'll never forget it. He was no more scared or white around the mouth or nothing. He screwed down and got both reins in one hand and said, "Let me feel of him." And then he screamed and jobbed that old thing, and you talk about tearing one up! He just cleaned his flues out.

And Boots won the heart of every cowboy out there that day. They respected that little guy. He had nerve and he had ability. And was a good cowboy. His old daddy was a heck of a cowboy.

All the people who drawed wages at the JA weren't cowboys. Most of them were but some weren't. When they needed people, they hired people and took their word that they were good hands. While I was out there, I'll bet I saw seventy-five cowboys come and go. Some of them were crackerjack hands and some were fellows who just needed a little moving-around money.

I worked for the JA's three years at different times. I never did winter but part of one winter. That got tough. I didn't like that wintertime business.

When we were out with the wagon, we were there seven days a week. I've gone as high as two months without going to town. When we did go to town, sometimes we'd ride our horses to the nearest camp and the camper would take us to town. Sometimes people came out.

Some of those older cowboys had pickups or cars. If we got close enough to headquarters, one of them might ride over and get his car and take it to the wagon and load a bunch of us up. But that didn't happen very often.

The bookkeeper's name was Glen Churchman. He had a jeep and he'd come out to the wagon and pick up our laundry, take it and get it done, and hold it out of our wages. If you needed something from the ranch store, he'd write it down and keep track of it—cigarettes, chewing tobacco, or a new saddle blanket. Next time he came out, he'd bring it to you.

At that time, the best Navaho saddle blanket cost twelve dollars. You couldn't get one for $112 today, the kind we got.

That bookkeeper would come to the wagon every day or every other day, and he'd bring our mail. They had their own post office—Palo Duro, Texas. If the cook ran out of anything, Glen would bring it.

We killed a 350-pound heifer every other day at the wagon. The cook would keep what he needed and what wouldn't spoil, maybe a hindquarter, and send the rest to the commissary. They would distribute it to the ten camp men. The campers would go into headquarters to get their beef.

They also raised hogs, so we had ham and bacon.

One time in the middle of June, we were camped at the mouth of Campbell Creek. We got up in the morning and the mosquitoes were so thick you could hear a constant hum in the air—clouds of mosquitoes, mosquitoes everywhere. It was terrible, and this went on for ten days.

When we turned out the horses, they wouldn't graze or anything, they'd just stand on top of a hill to get away from the mosquitoes. When you went out on the drive, you couldn't put two fingers down on your horse without touching a mosquito. In the heat of summer, we had to wear gloves and even wore flour sacks over our heads. At night, we'd burn those old cedar trees to smoke 'em out. They were in the food, they got into your bedroll at night, they were everywhere.

One morning I got up to use the bathroom, and I thought, boy, I'd better slam this tarp down before it gets full of those mosquitoes—but there weren't any. It was so quiet it shocked me. There was not one mosquito. Where they went, I don't know, 'cause they were there when we went to bed. I guess that was the most miserable time I ever spent anywhere.

In the spring, that wagon would leave headquarters around Easter, and in the fall, we stayed out until late in the season. As a matter of fact, sometimes there was snow on the ground. It would get pretty cold at night and we slept in tipis.

On a cold night, we'd get one of those Brer Rabbit syrup buckets and fill it with coals from the fire pit. We'd hang it by a wire from the top of the tipi, and in the morning it would be nice and warm in there.

Usually two men would sleep in one tipi, if they could get along well enough. We carried them in the bed wagon. The poles were made out of two pieces of pipe that were hinged at the top, and we rolled the stakes up in the canvas. They folded up pretty small. Those wooden stakes that came with it, they'd last about two licks with a sledge hammer, so we had some made out of steel.

Those tipis would keep the rain out, unless somebody messed with 'em—which we did all the time. See, with that old canvas, if you touched it during a rain, water would just pour inside, and we'd "go visiting" the neighbors' tipis and mess with them.

There was quite a bit involved in setting up a camp. I've often thought about all the things that went into those wagons. We'd have twenty-five or thirty stake ropes sixty feet long tied on the sides. We'd have twenty or twenty-five bedrolls in the bed wagon. Then they had a wagon they called the hoodlum wagon that carried water and wood. They carried the food and pots and the big canvas fly in the chuck wagon.

The older you got, the smarter you got when it came time for setting up camp. Those old lazy boys would say, "Aw, it ain't going to rain," and they wouldn't help set up the tipis. Then, if it did rain, they wanted in there. But the door flaps tied from the inside, so they didn't get in unless you wanted 'em in.

But if you didn't let 'em in, sometimes your tipi would fall in during the night.

People who've never worked around a wagon may not know it, but we had laws we went by. You didn't unsaddle your horse upwind from the wagon and let that hair blow in there.

In the first place, you didn't get within fifty yards of it. That was a no-no. You didn't ride up to the wagon, wherever the wind was blowing. You sure didn't unsaddle upwind from the wagon. If the wind was blowing pretty hard, you didn't tie one upwind of the wagon. Those old cooks would get you.

When I was working at the RO's, they had an old cook. He was crabby but I liked him immediately. I had a little old goosey dun horse. Somebody's horse had bucked him off and it run over there towards the wagon and I was going to head it off. This cook was pouring out his dishwater. He saw me coming and rolled that old washtub out there under my horse, and he bucked me off.

He said, "You know better than to bring a horse up close to my wagon."

I said, "I was trying to keep that other horse away from it."

He said, "Don't never ride a horse that close to my wagon."

Another time, I had a brand new set of bridle reins, just bought 'em. I rode my horse up there to the wagon and tied him to the wagon wheel. The cook never said a word, just got a butcher knife and cut them bridle reins right in the middle.

The JA wagon had their laws and you had to respect them. They had a court and the judge would sentence you: three licks with leggings, say. It depended on the seriousness of the charge.

I went to sleep on a drive one morning and every man there got two licks on my behind. We'd been to Clarendon the night before, come back into camp and never did go to bed. Bud Long told me to get the cattle out of that Hardscrabble Creek. It was kind of a compliment to me because that's where they usually got away and he felt I had the ability to keep them from doing it.

When I got over there, I tied my horse to a tree and got down and went to sleep. And here I looked up and there were about four of 'em, sitting on their horses and looking at me. That was one of the worst moments of my life. I knew I was in trouble. And sure enough, I was right. We lost just about all the cattle. I don't think we branded more than ten calves that morning.

But that taught me quite a bit about being dependable. It was very enlightening to a young man. Those kinds of things you don't forget.

There was this old dumb kid working out there one time. They were going to chap him. He got mad and backed up to that wagon and grabbed a butcher knife. They just ignored him until he settled down, and then they grabbed him and tied him to the wagon wheel and left him there all day.

The wagon boss told the cook, "Don't even talk to him. Let him wet in his britches."

And that's the way it happened. I'll guarantee you, that little feller never got mad again, or if he did, he didn't let anybody know about it. It was a powerful lesson for a young man, how to discipline his temper.

Like any bunch of cowboys, we played pranks on each other and found our ways of livening things up. One of our tricks was to take the lacing out of an old boy's stirrup leather, where it hooked on to the stirrup, and replace it with a piece of twine string.

When he'd put his weight on that stirrup, the string would break and it would scare the horse. Them old horses would sure try to take a swat at you.

And then we'd take the right stirrup off and hide it. The old boy would get into the saddle in the dark and punch around on the right side of that horse, looking for the stirrup. That would kind of wake those horses up too.

When we were out alone in hot weather, we'd drink out of windmills, ponds, or the river. Some of those wells had gyp water, and a man was better off not to drink out of them. It would work on you just like Epsom salts.

When we had a new kid on the crew, we'd keep him away from water until 2 or 3 in the afternoon and then go to one of them gyp wells. We'd drunk enough of it so that our systems had got used to it, but it would have an embarrassing effect on someone who wasn't used to it. That was one of our main pranks on a new kid.

I've already talked about how it was a chapping offense to tie a horse too close to the wagon. Well, these young blades would come out there and go to work for the ranch, and we'd wait until they were asleep or not watching and we'd tie their horses up next to the wagon.

That old cook would see it there, and the wreck was on!

We were all the time giving those cooks trouble. One morning on the drive, I was sitting there on my horse and looked down and saw what looked like red beans. They were little red rocks, and I got me a handful of them.

We'd already been torturing that cook about how he couldn't see, because one morning he looked at his clock and thought it was ten minutes after five, when it was really 2:25. He got up and started breakfast, and we hoo-rawed him over that, said he couldn't see.

When I found those rocks, I thought, "How fitting this would be!" When I went through the line, I dropped those rocks in the pot of beans and stirred 'em up. And of all things, the wagon boss came through behind me. And when those rocks hit his tin plate, we heard, "Ping, ping."

He never said a word, just got up and got that pot hook and hit me across the ribs with it. I tried to tell him that the cook couldn't see well enough to tell a bean from a rock, but he didn't go for that.

I worked another deal with James Owens, who later was a bootmaker in Clarendon. The wind was blowing eighty miles an hour and the cook was trying to make biscuits in them old dutch ovens. The wind made the fire too hot and it was kind of searing the biscuits. The crusts were about an inch thick on each side, and then they were raw in the middle. The cook was pretty concerned about it.

After we got through eating, I picked up a little stick and told James Owens, "When I bite into the biscuit, you break the stick." We called the cooks "coose " from the Spanish word "cocinero." I said, "Coose, could I have another one of those good biscuits?" He knew derned well something was in the wind.

He was washing out the coffee pot, and he said, "They're over on the chuckbox."

James was sitting on the tongue of the bed wagon and I went over and sat down beside him. That old cook was watching. He knew we were up to something. I bit into that biscuit and James broke the stick, and then I grabbed my jaw like I'd broke it.

Old Coose grabbed the coffee pot and I ran. There was kind of a slope there. He throwed that coffee pot and hit me in the hip with it, and just rolled me down that hill.

Grassburrs were everywhere! I was wearing a brand new vest. I scraped grassburrs out of that thing with my pocket knife for the longest time and finally just threw it away.

9

One time I came in to the wagon and dropped my rope on the ground. It was hotter than blazes and that was a good rope. I didn't want to leave it out in the sun.

When I dropped it, it stirred up a little dust but not enough to hurt anything. He never said a word, went over and got a cup of water out of the keg and poured it on my rope. Those old grass ropes would stiffen up, you know, when they got wet, and you could hardly throw one.

I said, "How come you did that?"

"I was wetting that ground so it wouldn't make any dust."

It made me mad. I grabbed that rope and swatted him up side the head with it, and I knew that I'd made a mistake.

He had an old nail keg that he sat on, had a pillow on top of it. I took off running and he threw that nail keg at me, knocked me down. I had my initials on the inside of the heel band of my spurs, and it knocked them off of one of them.

He said, "By God, you'll get hungry at lunch! What did you bring that rope in for anyway?"

"Well, it handles better. I can catch better."

He said, "You couldn't catch the clap in Ft. Worth with six hundred dollars."

The JA Horses

I never did break horses on the JA's. I wish I had. I would rather have ridden raw broncs than some of them we had to ride that had all this *knowledge*. They knew what to do and when to do it.

The JA's had some of the best horses in the world, but they weren't *made*. Now those bosses, they had some pretty good horses, and I was fortunate enough to have some pretty good horses when I left there. I had twenty-two horses in my string when I left there. About eight of them were bitted out—you could ride 'em with a bridle. The rest were broncs or older horses.

We furnished our own bridles. Most of us had only one bridle and one hackamore but we would borrow from each other to get the right kind of bit. Most of those old horses' mouths were ruined anyway. You had to use a short-shank bit in that brush. A longer one would hang and get you in a mess. The shank had to be shorter than the horse's mouth, and incidentally, you had no leverage on the horse.

When I say "hackamore," I mean a rawhide nose band with a headstall on it. If you had the nosepiece alone, you'd call it a bosal. If it's got reins on it, it's a hackamore.

They started a horse with a hackamore. They didn't really think you should put much stuff on one. They thought you ought to ride him to eight or nine years old before you started trying to make a cowhorse out of him. I'd always had a different opinion on that. I've had some two-year-olds that you could hold a pretty tough cow with, but it danged sure does damage their hocks and they'll get wind puffs, and by the time they're seven or eight, they're stiff in their shoulders.

Those old men knew what they were doing.

On the JA, you didn't spur a horse in front of that cinch and you didn't hit him in front of that cinch. When I went to work

11

for them, Mr. Bill Word talked to me. He was quiet and he was smart. He said, "Frankie, any horse you ride that JA brand off of, we'll give it to you. Anything behind that cinch is yours. Anything in front of it belongs to the ranch." You didn't reach up and slap a JA horse. Well, most of the time you didn't have nerve enough. If you got that much out of position, you was bucked off anyway.

If the management thought you were mistreating a horse, they always had twenty or thirty of these old things nobody wanted. If a boy went out there and got to jobbing around on a good horse to make him buck—they'd all buck if you fooled with them—next time they changed horses, he didn't have to job that horse. They kept those old horses around for that very purpose.

You respected those horses. You didn't lope them up a hill. They taught you right. You reserved that horse's stamina because you didn't know how long you'd have to ride him or where you might have to go.

But the thing I appreciated about the JA's more than anything was that each horse had a job. When we'd throw that roundup together, the horse wrangler was there with horses and he caught you a roundup horse. When you got through with the roundup, you changed horses again. That roundup horse, all he had to do was look at a cow. They saw to that.

On some other outfits, you'd catch one of these old things and they had been run down so many times, they were just killed out. You could get down on the ground and outrun him on a drive. But not the JA's. I've changed horses as many as five times a day, and you've got to respect that because they respected those horses.

They wouldn't break a horse until he was four years old, and their theory was correct. A two-year-old couldn't take the riding. A three-year-old was shedding his teeth and couldn't eat right and he'd get thin. When he got a four-year-old mouth, he could eat and take care of himself, because they rode those horses hard. They really did. Those were big old pastures and you'd leave in a lope and ride 'em plumb into the ground, chasing those crazy old cows.

I can't imagine taking any of my horses today on one of those deals.

At some of the JA camps, they had burros. Sometimes they were necked to wild cattle and led them out to a place where they could be reached with a truck. And sometimes the men would use the burros to halter-break broncs, neck the broncs to the burros. They'd get pretty hard to deal with.

They said this one old burro at the JA's—it might have been at Tom Blasingame's camp—they'd have to tie him and drag him up to a horse, and then tie him to the horse. That would be quite a chore. But you tie enough of them big old rank broncs to a burro and he gets to where he'll kick you. He don't want any of that.

The JA had big horses, a lot of them sixteen hands high. Them old Midnights and Gray Eagles, they had a big old wide cannon and you couldn't cripple one of them. The older horses were big horses. The younger ones, the King Georges and the Tom Adairs, weren't as big. But you couldn't keep a saddle on one of them Tom Adairs because they didn't have any withers, and you couldn't ride the King Georges because they were crippled all the time. Their legs weren't as big around as your wrist.

Most of those King Georges were roundup horses because they were derned sure cow horses. They would watch a cow. And they were treacherous. They weren't bad to buck, but they'd bite you or paw you or kick you. They weren't trustworthy.

Course, a lot of them weren't, and they didn't have any reason to be trustworthy. We'd take them off of their mothers and wean 'em, rope 'em and brand 'em and turn 'em out in the pasture. Then, when they was two-year-olds, we'd forefoot 'em and cut the studs and turn 'em out in that 120-section pasture. And they didn't even see a man until they were four-year-olds. Well, they'd get a glimpse of a man when we were gathering that pasture.

Then we'd get 'em in and forefoot 'em and put a hackamore on 'em and stake 'em. So they really didn't have any reason to think that a man was their friend. They was of the old wild instinct—survival—and they thought they was supposed to kill us, and they almost done it. I tell you what, there was always two or three men laying around the wagon or in the hospital, crippled by them horses.

Even the older horses had a wild instinct. When the wagon pulled in in the fall, we'd keep a few horses up for the winter and kick the rest of them out in the pasture to fend for themselves. Then, in April, we got them up and tried to ride them. It was pretty entertaining, more so for other people than for me because I always seemed to have quite a few crazy old things. I wasn't smart enough to say no.

But I sure learned a lot of things about a horse out there. I couldn't always ride 'em. They could buck me off any time they wanted to. Now, a green one that was bucking because he was scared, I could usually ride him unless he was exceptionally rank. But one of them old things that would hit over here and then over here, and then kind of stop and look back at you, now, they bucked me off.

In the fall, when we were delivering cattle on the river, they'd send two men into the remuda to rope out the horses and stake 'em. Bud Long and Jiggs Mann usually did the roping. Each cowboy would tell the ropers what he wanted to ride for the day. I've helped. You'd just have to skylight those horses because it was still dark. I knew them by their ears and the tops of their heads.

Usually they had 300 to 350 head of horses in the remuda. Bud Long and Jiggs Mann knew every horse by name. After I'd been there two months, I knew every horse by name, who rode him, who his daddy was. I've always had a pretty good memory about horses. Each one has a different personality, like people, and something about him, if you're looking for it, will make you remember him.

I have ridden broncs that were two- or three-year-olds and sold them, and when I saw them again when they were seven or eight, something about them looked familiar. They didn't look the same as when I saw them last, but I was able to recognize them.

Any time you're involved with numerous horses, there are going to be unfortunate things that happen to them, and ninety percent of the time it happens to the best horse on the place. I remember there was the nicest little bronc in the remuda called Gold Dollar. Jack Ray had been riding him. He was a little old skinny thing and nobody had wanted to ride him. Nobody had ridden him since he'd left the bronc pen, but Jack saw something in him he liked and went to riding him, and it wasn't two months until that was the cowingest thing on the outfit.

Well, one night a mountain lion or something scared those horses and ran them through a fence, and of course Gold Dollar was the one that got cut up the worst. He'd probably outrun everything else. We were going to have to kill him. I think there were twenty-four men with the wagon, plus Bud Long, the wagon boss. Bud had this Winchester and he went around to everybody, looking for somebody who'd go kill that horse. Nobody would, so he left there saying, "I never seen such a bunch of chicken-livered sons of bucks!" Directly we heard a shot and Bud never showed up. I went out there after a while to see about him, and he was sitting over there crying.

Most cowboys I know can kill anything but a horse.

While I was with the JA's, I had a little old horse called Billy Roan, and I knew he could run. I kept talking about how fast he was, and one day Floyd Freeman said he bet he had a horse that could outrun mine. I said, "I ain't got any money but I'll bet you my saddle."

He said he didn't want to run his horse very far, just fifty yards, and I said all right.

Well, Billy could sure run. They used to take him to Clarendon and run him a quarter-mile, and they won every time with him. They had an old gray horse named Ashtola that won all the cuttings, and Billy Roan won the quarter-mile races.

So this horse had proven that he could run. Floyd's horse was called Capitan, and he wasn't famous for being fast. But Floyd knew horses, and he won my saddle. I was sick. I asked him if I could borrow it until payday, when I could get me another one, and he let me.

I couldn't understand how Floyd had beat me, so I asked him about it. He said, "I knew Capitan could beat your horse in fifty yards. He couldn't have won running seventy-five but I knew he could win at fifty yards. Capitan's hocks are closer to the ground and he can get away from the start and be gone. A horse with his hocks close to the ground can do things quick."

He let me worry about losing my saddle. I'd already made arrangements to get another one. He'd see me and say, "Now, don't put my saddle on that crazy thing, don't let him kick my saddle." He let me sweat right up to the end and then he gave it back to me.

That was a valuable lesson I learned about a horse's hocks. You go to a steer roping or a tripping and the horses that win have short canon bones. They're powerful, they can pull.

"That was in '47, I believe . . ..
I was just home from the JA's."

Two Bad Ones:
Twilight and Blaze

When I went to work on the JA's, they gave every man ten older horses and two broncs. It didn't matter whether you rode 'em or not, they were in your string. The older men would hire a younger cowboy to ride their broncs but they still had them in their mount.

I'd just got there and I didn't have any broncs yet. We were cutting out horses to go down to the river and I noticed that this four-year-old horse was running with the work horses. The cowboys called him "that old crazy Figure 2 brown," and they said, "We ought to just kill him. He ain't no count." I asked the wagon boss about him. He said the horse was a bronc and nobody wanted him.

They'd never finished breaking him. He'd jump out of those corrals and go run with the work horses at headquarters. He was an athlete.

I said, "Well, I'm supposed to have a bronc. I'll take him." I had no idea what I was saying, and I seen all those cowboys looking at me and I thought, "Hmm." But it just made it more definite that I was going to keep him.

A while later, the wagon boss come around and said, "Son, you don't have to keep that horse. He might cripple you." And I said, "Well, we'll see about that."

When we got down to that first wagon camp on the river, there were some big branding pens there, and I said, "Let's see about this brown horse." It took me twenty minutes to get a hackamore on him. They had to forefoot him and throw him down. He'd just eat you. You can't believe how he hated a man.

With the help of some of those old boys, I got his hind foot tied up and got him saddled. I knew how to do all those things, you know, but I'd never faced one before that thought his first job on earth was to see that I was dead.

I got on him and rode him around in that branding pen. He didn't buck, he just kicked at my feet. We were doing all right, so I said, "Let me out. I've got his number." Out was a seventy-seven thousand–acre pasture.

Well, they turned us out and he went to bucking. Of course, I was going to ride him. I squatted down pretty close to him and got a rein in each hand. He went two or three jumps, bucked over there and broadsided a mesquite tree. I got off, you might say, and he got away in that 120-section pasture. With my saddle.

I only had one saddle. They usually carried an extra but somebody was already using it. I had to lay around that wagon for several days—embarrassed. Three or four days later, they located the horse and got him back.

I named him Twilight, and old Twilight was learning faster than I was.

I'd have to hobble him to saddle him, and one time I tied one end of my rope to the hobbles and the other end to the bottom of a post. I got him saddled and threw a stirrup leather in the air. He whirled and took off and stuck his nose in the ground. After that, you didn't have to put hobbles on him, just wrap a hackamore rein around his legs and he wasn't going to leave.

When I got on him, he'd kick at my feet, and when my leggings flopped, he'd kick at them. He could kick both spurs down over the heels of my boots at the same time. When a mesquite got hung on the flank cinch and whacked him, he'd just kick it to death. I couldn't get up and down on him without somebody helping me. When I had to go to the bathroom or something, I'd have to go to Bud Long, the drive leader at the time, and get him to help me. He'd carry me around with him on the outside circle and keep an eye on me. I'd go to him when I wanted to get down and he'd say, "You need to use the bathroom, ha, ha, ha!"

I'd pitch him a hackamore rein and he'd dally it around his horn. Then he'd take his brush jacket off and put it over old Twilight's head, and I'd get down and take care of my business.

After I'd ridden him a while, I switched him over from a hackamore to a bridle. One time, heck I'd been riding him a year and a half, I was adjusting the bridle and it kind of popped. That sucker kicked me, just rolled me out there!

Twilight never would have made a bucking horse, and I don't know why he didn't buck harder. He was athletic enough. I guess the Lord was trying to protect me. As a matter of fact, he only bucked with me two times. The first time was when he went into that mesquite tree. The second time I rode him, he went into a mesquite tree again and stopped. I decided to give him a whipping for it. Of course, on the JA's you didn't hit a horse in front of that front cinch. They had a lot of respect for their horses and they took good care of them. They had a lot more respect for their horses than they did for their cowboys.

But my rope string had come undone in the tree and I took my rope down and went to whipping on his head. It was still dark by then and I knew nobody could see me.

He throwed his head up and broke my nose. My nose swole up and I could barely see around it. Later, some of the boys said, "Well, there's no way that horse could have missed your nose, big as it is."

I guess some of the boys thought I was taking too much abuse from old Twilight. One time this feller—I won't call his name but he was a reputable cowboy—he told me, "I used to have a horse a whole lot like that. He'd buck me off every time I got on him, but I figured out a way to fix him. You can drop some buckshot in one of his ears, boy, and in about a week, you won't have to fool with him any more. I've done it."

The buckshot works its way through the ear into the brain, and it'll kill him.

That same man said he'd also unsaddled a bad bronc, cut his throat, and shoved him off a bluff before he fell down. He was a tough old bird. He didn't talk much, but when he did, you thought about it. Sometimes it took you three days to figure out what he meant.

I often wondered what a man of his caliber and with a mind as intelligent as he had was doing out there, drawing ninety dollars a month as a cowboy. I found out later that he had been quite a reputable person and he'd gotten in a little trouble. He was just trying to make himself scarce. I knew there had to be a reason for him being there. He had ability and knowledge. He could have been running the outfit.

I finally got Twilight where I could get up and down on him. It was in the second year I was there, and he'd been turned out all winter. As usual, it took three men to saddle him. You'd just go to him with the saddle and he'd kick it out of your hands. And I promised him, "Little feller, you ain't getting this saddle off until you learn to stand there."

I rode him three days in a row without taking that saddle off. During that three-day deal, them other cowboys might have changed horses twelve times and I only rode him. You could take the fire out of a horse on that old JA.

When I finally pulled the saddle, there was a patch of hide the size of your hand came off each kidney. I hadn't thought about that happening and I couldn't ride him for two months, until his back got well. And I didn't doctor him. You didn't get that far back on him and live through it. Lord, he would have loved that, me putting meat grease on his back!

But that's when I got him to where I could get up and down on him.

He was some kind of horse. I'd like to have him today and start over on him. He was one of the most athletic horses I've ever ridden. But he never became an honest horse. He'd give you a hundred percent if you'd ask for it, he'd run until he fell dead. He never would quit. He was honest that way. But when you were on the ground, he was sure dishonest.

Well, maybe not. Maybe he was honest then too. You were supposed to be smart enough not to get into a vulnerable position with him where he could do something to you, because he would do it. And I guess he was honest about it.

He became a good horse. He'd watch a cow and I roped a lot on him. One time we'd moved a bunch of cattle and were going back to the wagon when I saw this old cow with nice horns, and I thought, "I bet I can rope her a hundred times out of a hundred."

When we were in that brush, we'd shake out a loop and it would figure-eight and we'd put it under our arm to keep it from snagging in the brush. When we hit an opening, we'd bring it up and feed a coil into it and it would open.

I had my loop fixed under my arm and we got after that old cow and we hit some old washed-out trails. I didn't see them and Twilight didn't either. He fell down and I went way out there, and when I quit rolling, I had that rope around me. And I thought, "Brother, this is IT."

But that horse had really hit hard on his head. He had dirt all over him and in his eyes, and he was kind of stumbling around. That gave me enough time to get out of the loop. But if it had knocked me out and he'd got his wits about him, we wouldn't be writing this book.

After that, I petted him one time. But I didn't pet him much. He'd have thought that was a sign of weakness. Boyd Rogers, the man who taught me so much about horses, had told me that some horses like to be petted and some horses like to be left alone. You do what you have to do with them and no more. Twilight was one of those, and I found it out pretty quick. He was just kind of a loner.

The only affection he had for me was hoping that some day I'd make a mistake. I'm still here today, so I guess I didn't make the one he was waiting for.

He never was trustworthy. You never got behind that stirrup. You didn't drop your reins and go to trimmin' his feet. As a matter of fact, he trimmed his own feet. I didn't. And if one broke off at the quick, I just enjoyed it all that much more.

But he wasn't the only one that would kick and paw. All those young JA horses would. After a while some of the older horses became more civilized. But any of them, if you moved quick in front of them, they'd paw you. It was their nature.

21

That's the way they was raised. But Twilight was the worst of all of them. He's the worst I've ever dealt with, before or since.

When I left there, he was making a good horse. You still couldn't treat him like another horse but his attitude had improved.

But one morning, after I'd left the ranch, he got a stake rope between his ears. When he did that, you did not approach him or he'd kill you. What you'd do is go behind him and directly he'd move up. But this particular morning, a cowboy went by him and busted him on the butt with some bridle reins. He was at the end of a sixty-foot stake rope. He got astraddle of it and started running.

By the time he hit the end of it, he'd been going 120 feet, and in 120 feet Twilight could be totin' the mail. He hit the end of it and did something to his back. The last time I saw him, he was in those railroad pens at Clarendon, going to the killers. Three of my old horses were in that bunch: Twilight, Stupid, and an old gray horse called Diddy-Wah-Diddy.

It was kind of sad. I thought of all the hell me and Twilight had been through, and him to end up like that. It made me sad.

One time on the JA's they sent me from one end of that ranch to the other, from Antelope Flat nearly to Claude. They had about eleven sections up on the plains and I was to go up there and help a man doctor screwworms.

The man who was up there was named Sid McElroy. A team had run away with him the winter before. The kingpin bounced out of the doubletree and the tongue stuck in the ground and wrecked the wagon. It broke Sid's back.

So I went up on the plains to help him. It was about thirty miles, I guess. I was riding Twilight. I was getting along pretty well with him. I could get up and down on him, but I couldn't lead him through a gate. And I'll bet I had to go through twenty-five gates. I had to shake my hat in his face and back him through and hope he didn't get loose.

About five o'clock that evening I was feeling sorry for him. He hadn't had a drink and I hadn't either. I rode him up to one of those concrete water tanks. My foot rubbed on the side of it and he kicked at it, knocked a quarter off his hind hoof. Crippled him. I was wishing it had been the left one, the one he was always trying to use on me.

When I got there, Sid gave me a couple of horses to use, since I'd crippled old Twilight. But I saw another horse around there. He was a big red dun, bald face, two white legs, as good-looking a dun horse as I'd ever seen. He was just a cowboy's dream. I asked Sid who that was, and he said, "Blaze."

I'd heard them cowboys talking about a horse called Blaze, the buckingest horse on the place. He had that reputation. There was one in the remuda called Cimarron that was a pitchin' jewel, but them old cowboys said, "He can't go like that Blaze horse."

Sid asked if I wanted to ride him and I said, "Well, yeah, I guess so." So he caught him. He was one of the few you didn't have to rope. Sid just walked up to him and caught him.

I saddled him and started to lead him off, and Sid said, "Wait just a minute." He come over there and tied the bridle reins around his neck and ran his thumbnail down that horse's shoulder, and I'd never seen such pitching and bawling and carrying on.

I said, "Sid, is there any way we can get my saddle off that son of a gun before he tears it to pieces?"

He said, "No, he'll be all right. You've got to let him play a while or he'll sure buck you off. Or he might not buck *you* off but he does most people."

He had a big old docile eye and a nice head. He didn't have a bucking horse head. If I had judged him strictly by his head and eye, I would have missed. But he wasn't dishonest about it. He'd tell you four steps before he cut loose that he was going to buck, so you could go to looking for a nice place to land.

Heck, I rode him all the time I was up there, about three weeks. The worms were terrible and they were bringing new cattle up there all the time. And that old horse made a good horse for me.

Sid was like a lot of other cowboys. They just rode a horse. They didn't spend much time settin' one down and turning him around. They just did what they had to do. But I worked with him and, say, this old thing could lock in and turn around.

When I got ready to leave, Sid said, "Frankie, I think you ought to have that horse. Take him on. After you've got him tired, he won't buck with you."

Sid gave him to me and I led him back down to the wagon and throwed him in with the remuda. Them older cowboys knew what he was and the younger ones had heard about him, and when they saw me bringing in old Blaze, they looked at me in a different light.

But what neither one of us had thought of—I sure as heck hadn't, Sid might have—was that when I was out with the wagon, there wasn't any place to turn him a-loose in the morning to get the bucking out of his system. We were working in that hundred-twenty–section pasture, with no pens anywhere.

Well, I didn't ride him for several days. Then I caught him one day to round up on and say, this sucker sure did buck me off, pretty severely. That Blaze was the kind that loved affection. You could scratch the end of his ears and under his chin and he liked it, but that didn't change his instinct that he was supposed to buck me off.

I kept him around. He bucked me off four or five times, is all. He never made one jump in the same direction as the last one. I believe he was National Finals material. That old thing could get in more different shapes! Even old Will James couldn't have drawn a picture of him. And he made all kinds of noise. It kind of unnerved you, whether you could ride him or not.

I kind of figured out how to get on him and keep him going in a circle until he quit groaning.

One time I roped a cow on him, and that old sucker just whomped and turned back and got the rope over the top of my leggings, and he was bucking, dragging that cow, or he would have bucked me off then. He didn't spin or turn that time. He bucked straight out, which was something he never did.

When I left the JA's, there was a young fellow who wanted Blaze. I asked the wagon boss about it and he said, "Yeah, I think he ought to have him." This boy could ride a bucking horse. I won't call his name and embarrass him, but he was a better bronc rider than I was. He *wanted* 'em to buck. I didn't. He was wanting to make a bronc rider, and he sure as thunder did make a bronc rider.

But I heard later that the dust was still in the air from my leaving when Blaze bucked him off.

I knew it was going to happen. I just wish I'd seen it.

The Hedgecoke Ranch

When I went to work for Hedgecokes, they took me to the headquarters there at Goodnight, Texas. They had thirteen milk cows and I think I milked six of them. They had twenty or thirty dogie calves to put on the other milk cows, and I had to do that too. I ran the milk through a separator. They saved the cream and fed the milk to seventy-five head of hogs. This went on for about ten days, and finally I told that foreman, "Look, I've got too much money tied up in leather to be milking them danged old cows. If you can't put me ahorseback, you take me to the boot shop in Clarendon and let me off."

So he took me to the ranch they had down in Palo Duro Canyon. They had a ranch house and bunk house down there, and a kind of semi-foreman who ran things. They'd move the cowboys around to the Goodnight ranch and they had some country over by Wayside, on the south rim of the canyon.

They branded on the shoulder, and when he took me down there, I bet I saw twenty head of calves with screwworms in those brands. The next morning we were going to gather the pasture and doctor worms. This old foreman, his name was Hobart Brace, he had a big old bay horse named Cider. They put me on some old thing that couldn't do nuthin'.

Hobart had both hands on the reins, holding Cider. He was taking little steps and humping along, and I just eased up there and roped that horse by the heels. He didn't buck Hobe off, but he sure done a little number out there. Hobe never said a word, but directly we were riding along and he eased up beside me and said, "Don't ever do that again." And I didn't.

Hobe was a real good man. I'd ride them old bad horses that nobody else wanted to ride and I tried to make him a good hand. Most of those cowboys didn't like fence work. I didn't like it either but I figured I was drawing their wages so I ought to do what they wanted done. To me, doing things ahorseback had priority over everything else.

I met Coyote Morris when I was working for Hedgecokes. Now, there was an *interesting man*. He must have been about thirty-five when I knew him. He come from Falfurrias, Texas. He was an orphan boy and was raised by an old rancher down there named Ed Rochelle. Ed had racehorses and wound up with a Derby winner named Equipoise.

Coyote grew up on Ed's ranch, and he could speak Spanish just like English. When they had that hoof and mouth disease in Mexico, he went there and was working for the government. He killed an old boy down there and they took his citizenship papers away from him.

He was a single man and he'd gotten acquainted with this pretty Mexican lady. He didn't know she had a husband. She never mentioned it. A friend told Coyote she was married and he quit having anything to do with her. But one night he was in a bar and a Mexican guy come in there with a little pistol in his left hand.

A friend of Coyote's punched him and said, "That's him." The Mexican crossed himself and looked Coyote right square in the eye, and Coyote knew he'd come for a killing, so Coyote shot him. Coyote told me, "I just had an instinct that he was going to kill me. It was something that shouldn't have happened, but it did."

He'd get to talking about it and he'd cry and say that he was a man without a country and couldn't vote. I told him, "Well, you can breathe. There's no use to feel so bad. You're making these Hedgecokes a good hand. People love you and respect you. I do." And I'd get him settled down.

He was an artist with a pistol. He had an old forty-five that had belonged to Poncho Villa's right-hand man and, oh, he was proud of that pistol! He had a .357 magnum that he carried with him in the pasture. Why? Because he was Coyote. One time I saw him shoot the head off a road runner at seventy-five yards.

One time he went back to Iowa with a load of fat cattle and he met a lady. She was fascinated with him because he was a cowboy and they didn't see many Texas cowboys. He told her that he owned the JA ranch. She said she was wealthy too. He told me, "I thought I'd tell her what she wanted to hear, but what I didn't know was that she was telling me stories too."

They wrote letters to each other, and then she said she was coming to Texas to see his ranch, and he told her to come on. He was living in a camp way down in Palo Duro Canyon and making ninety dollars a month as a cowboy, and come to find out, she was a school teacher and didn't have no money either.

They got married at Clarendon and he moved her down to his camp, but their deal didn't work out too good. They got into a squabble one night and he shot all her grandmother's tea cups off the wall. He hadn't read the Dale Carnegie book, and she didn't stay around very long. He always felt bad about that.

He was pleasant to be around—until you hot-footed him, and then he made you wish you were a hundred miles away. I did that *once*. It was after the Fourth of July, I believe, and Coyote had gotten these new shark-skin boots. He wasn't really used to drinking. He didn't drink very often but he'd gotten a little too much over the holiday. I believe July the Fourth was on Saturday and we was supposed to be back out at the ranch on Sunday the fifth.

About four o'clock in the afternoon on Sunday, we were in the bunkhouse. The windows didn't have any shades on them and the sun was coming through the big west window and shining on those new boots. He had picked them up the day before. Pete Borden had made them. Coyote was moving his foot around in his sleep and I knew that tight instep was biting him.

So I squirted a little lighter fluid around the sole and set it afire. And directly he came out of that bed and he was wanting to harm somebody. There were five or six of us in there, but he was pretty sure who did it.

He said, "These boots cost me a month's cowboy wages and I had to wait six months to get 'em." He talked about gettin' his six-shooter if that ever happened again, which it didn't. I was scared of him. He'd hurt you. I knew he'd killed people.

There was another story about Coyote. One day we was out and he was riding this old horse named Black Magic. There were some trails going off a caprock at an angle. It didn't just go straight off, you know. He was trying to beat some cattle to those trails, but they all got there at the same time.

He couldn't stop Black Magic, bailed him off that caprock and high-centered him in a cedar tree down below. He went to hollering for help. It was a pretty scary-looking deal. Coyote climbed down but the horse was still hung up in the tree. We had to go get an axe and chop the tree down to get him out.

It punched holes in the old horse. He wasn't much count anyway but he lived. He was still there when I left.

But the scariest deal I got into with Coyote, even scarier than when he offered to shoot me, was the time he was going to rope this two-year-old stud. He belonged to the neighbors and he'd got in there, been in there about all his life.

Coyote said, "They don't even know they've got him and he'd make a good horse and I'm going to catch him."

The grandmothers of those Hedgecoke horses were Spanish mares and their grandfather was a government stud, so they were half Spanish mare and half Thoroughbred. They bred the fillies out of this union back to a purebred Arabian horse. And let me tell you something: Nine men couldn't stay awake long enough to get one of them tired. They could run all day and they were just wonderful horses.

Boy, those horses could run! And they had a lot of sense. They weren't mean. They were just smart and wild and resented a man. They were a good cross and I wouldn't mind having some of them today—if I had a good horsebreaker around.

But like most of them old ranch horses, they weren't handled any except when you were going to do some work. Nobody spent any extra time with them.

And Coyote was breaking one of them colts. That's what he was riding. This was a three-year-old, I guess, and I know he hadn't rode him ten saddles. He'd broke his old rope up and it was about twenty-five foot long, and we jumped these horses up on this divide. They weren't really running, they were just kind of trotting off, and Coyote said, "I'm going to go get that two-year-old."

He took off and they beat him to the caprock, or they might have gotten there about the same time. That old thing I was on—Half Pint, we called him—was running away and acting ignorant and I was trying to keep my mind on him.

Anyway, when I got to the caprock there wasn't no slowing down or pulling up. All I could see there was a cloud of dust boiling up where Coyote and all them horses had gone off. Off I went, and it seemed like fifteen seconds I was in the air and couldn't see anything. I knew I'd be dead as soon as we hit the ground.

Directly, that old horse hit, and when the dust cleared, old Coyote had that stud colt roped by one front foot, and he might have caught him in the air. He was pretty western. He'd tried to catch both forefeet but his rope wasn't long enough and he only caught the right one.

The colt crossed over the rope and when Coyote tripped him down, it broke the colt's shoulder. When I got there, Coyote was trying to beat him to death with a mesquite root. It kind of made me sick to see that. I was going to help him, but he said, "I've got him. Go on and get that other colt. You look a little white around the mouth anyway."

This Half Pint horse I was riding, he was a fat, cute little thing, wouldn't weigh a thousand pounds. He was one of those that could kick you while you were putting the bridle on. Well, Coyote had roped himself a colt and there was another one that went off by himself, and I decided I might as well catch me one too.

I went after him but Half Pint couldn't catch him. I've roped a lot of loose horses, but you've got to have a handle on it. You don't just jump in behind them and run up on them. If you can catch one like that, he ain't worth putting your rope on in the first place.

I finally decided I wasn't going to catch that colt, so I bent Half Pint around and headed him into a bluff to get him stopped. He'd run so far his old mouth was numb. I was only about a mile from the horse pasture by then and I decided to go on without Coyote. I didn't want to see him right then anyway. I was kind of mad at him for what he'd done to that colt.

So I went on to the horse pasture gate. I'd never had to spur Half Pint to make him go, and now he was just barely moving. I got to feeling sorry for him. He was breathing hard and still pretty hot, so I unsaddled him and walked him around the way you do a polo pony to cool him out.

But then when I went to saddle him again, I couldn't do it. I had to tie his foot up to get a saddle on him.

Another time when I was riding Half Pint, the river was up and they couldn't get groceries to the wagon on the other side. I just happened to be around when they showed up in the pickup. They'd been through this many times before and had come prepared. They had put all the groceries in tow sacks so that they could be carried across the river on horseback.

When I reached and got that sack of groceries on Half Pint, things went to happening. He didn't buck. He just ran away and whirled and tried to get away from that sack.

I never made it to the river. That stuff was scattered all up and down that river. It took us twenty minutes to gather all that stuff up. Half Pint didn't believe in carrying groceries, and he didn't care if we had anything to eat or not.

After I left Hedgecokes, Coyote worked on one ranch and then another. He'd get homesick for South Texas and go down there. There's a little town on the Mexican border called Piedras Negras. He mentioned it a lot and named a horse after it. It was a special place to him. One morning he'd be gone to Piedras Negras.

A friend told me that Coyote bought a buffalo and he was riding it and training it. He started up to Canada. I think he was going to Calgary or somewhere, and he went through a customs station in Montana. They stopped him and checked his buffalo and said it had some kind of disease—and they killed it. And he killed two of those border boys, and the rest of them caught him and hung him.

That's what I heard, and I have every reason in the world to believe it, knowing Coyote.

31

Good Cowboys, Bad Cattle

I've had the good fortune of being around a lot of good cowboys. One time C. H. Long said something, and I think it's one of the better expressions about a cowboy. He said, "A cowboy is a person that can drive two yearling steers through a bunch of cows and calves, and have another one on the end of his rope." Now *that is a cowboy.*

I learned how to rope when I was growing up in Memphis, Texas. I'd throw at an empty coffee can and I got to where I could catch it a hundred times out of a hundred, but I'd never roped anything alive until I went to work for the JA's. There, I roped things that were quite a bit alive.

The JA's didn't frown on roping, the way people would today. We'd have to drive cattle fifteen to eighteen miles and we'd just rope all the way. We didn't rope much when we were working off the river. They had those campers that took care of the cattle off the river and it was an act of courtesy, you might say, that we didn't rope their cattle. But down on the river, those were the wildest old things anyway, and you couldn't hurt them. They were already ruined, you couldn't gather them.

The JA's bought their rope by the coil. It was a seven-six-teenths–inch True Blue silk manila rope. Boys, them was good-feeling ropes. But some of them old horses had learned that if they set down hard after you'd roped something big, they could break the rope right up there at the honda.

When we broke a rope, we'd tell Bill Word, the foreman, and he'd bring us a new one from headquarters. One time he noticed that he was bringing me quite a few. One evening before he left, he said, "You're sure using a lot of ropes." I told him that I was training on my horses, and with those old things you just broke a lot of ropes.

Those were big old horses and we were roping big cattle. Sometimes you'd come up with the short end around a tree and you'd want to give part of it to the cow—cut it a-loose. I gave two or three ropes away like that.

So Mr. Word said, "I'm going to bring you one in the morning, and that's the last one." He brought me one, and instead of eating breakfast that morning, I tied me a honda in one end of it. That day, I had two or three old cows turn back on the drive and I had to rope them. I had one that went around a tree and I couldn't get that old horse to move up. He was scared of the cow. I had to cut my rope to get out of that, and that shortened it a little bit.

Then I caught another one and tripped it, and it broke the rope where it went through the honda. That cost me another four or five feet. When I got to the roundup ground, my rope wasn't but eighteen or twenty feet long. When it was time to catch fresh horses, we threw our ropes to one another and made a circle of men and ropes around the remuda. Of all people who would be next to me, it was Bill Word! I threw that little rope out there to him. He didn't say anything, just reached down and got it.

He had the coldest blue eyes. When he wanted to look at you, he could look plumb through you. That's what he did then. I didn't ask for a new rope, and I carried that thing the rest of the day. It wasn't even long enough to drag calves with.

Well, in three or four days he brought me another one. I guess he figured out that I wasn't trying to break those ropes, that I was using them to train their horses.

We'd usually finish our roundup work by noon, and in the heat of the day we'd sit around those waterholes and wait for those old wild cattle to come in out of the brush. We all carried branding rings and a horn saw. We'd catch one, tie him down, brand him and saw his horns off, cut him if he was a bull, and turn him loose.

Those cattle were called mavericks. That's what they told me they were. Those old wild cattle were amazing. I have seen them unloaded from a truck and they would stand right there and die!

We usually handled them in the wintertime when it was cold. They was fat, looked like feedlot cattle. Now, a lot of people wouldn't believe that we had steers that weighed sixteen hundred to eighteen hundred pounds, but it's true, we did. And if you'd tell 'em that you used to rope and tie them down on a bronc, they wouldn't believe that either. But we did.

And I can guarantee you that they wouldn't hit the end of that rope over twice before here they'd come. All you'd have to do was leave the rope laying there and ease on out and pull their front feet out from under them. If you really busted one of them old big fat ones, he'd die, he'd never get up. You had to ease them down or tie 'em to a tree.

We always carried shackles. That's a short piece of rope with a horn loop in each end. Sometimes we tied the cattle down, sometimes we tied them to a tree and came back with help. Two of us would lead one out. I've heard about an old boy who would notch their horns and wrap wire around the horns and put a stick in the wire and twist it, the way you do on a fence corner. They say the cattle handle better with that. They won't come as near to locking up on you.

We had an old bobtail truck we used to pick up cattle we had tied down. The old man who drove the truck had him a Japanese flag with rings in the corners. When we were ready to load a cow that had locked down, he'd run the rope through those rings and slide the flag down the rope toward the cow. And here she'd come, after that flag.

I've been by myself when one locked up and I needed to take him to a place where they could get to it in the truck. I'd take my brush jacket and run the rope through one sleeve, and he'd go to it. He'd get it down and wallow it around. A man learns to use his head when he's out alone.

I was riding an old horse one time. I called him Stupid. He wouldn't look at you. They'd rope him and drag him out of the remuda, and he'd be looking way off, like he was seeing something. He wouldn't look at you, but when you touched him, the wreck was on. He'd blow sky high, paw you, do anything. So I named him Stupid. I kind of wanted him because of his daddy.

I'd rode him ten or twelve times. The wagon had just pulled out and it was still cold of a morning. I decided I'd take old Stupid down on the river and rope something. I knew where there was a windmill and figured there'd be some cattle we'd missed.

So, sure enough, here come a two-year-old heifer. There was still a little chill in the air and I had my neckerchief on and my jacket. I'd never roped anything on Stupid and I was by myself, and here came that two-year-old heifer with a perfect set of horns. I eased around and got between her and the thicket and headed her toward the river. I wanted to let her get full of water where she couldn't run so fast. I didn't have all that much control of this horse. I ran up on the heifer and Stupid ran past her when I went to slinging that rope, and I missed her. She went into the thicket and I went in and got her out and roped her. I tripped her down and broke off one horn.

I had spent three or four evenings building this good four-plait pigging string, with a leather burner in the honda. I was proud of it and I'd never used it before. I tied her down with it.

We was way out in the riverbed and I had to gather up wood to make a branding fire. I was gathering up sticks and old driftwood. There was one little mesquite bush out there, and I took off my neckerchief and hung it on that bush.

I had took my rope loose from the heifer and had Stupid's hackamore rein tied into the loop of my rope so I could keep him around. He'd been staked and he wouldn't challenge a stake rope. I got me a little fire going and had my branding ring in it. I don't know why, but I just happened to look back over my shoulder and that crazy heifer wasn't eighteen inches away from me. She had blood dripping off the end of her nose and I saw how sharp her horns were, and I thought, "You're a dead cowboy." At that time, that was the worst scare I'd ever had.

She was fixing to get me. She just stood there looking at me. I didn't move, even to breathe. A little breath of wind come along and moved that neckerchief on the bush. It kind of wiggled and she went after it. My good pigging string had come untied, I don't know why, and it was still tied on her front foot.

Then she went charging over and hit old Stupid, and she happened to hit him with the horn that had been broke off, or she'd have gutted the little son of a buck. She hit him and went on, and I laid down. I just gave her that pigging string and she stayed a maverick.

Another time, me and Stupid roped a wild cow and went on opposite sides of a mesquite tree. When that happened, if you had the shorter end of the rope, you were in bad trouble, because the cow had enough slack to get you. This time I had the longer end, but this old cow pulled my horse up to the tree and went to hooking Stupid on the shoulder. She didn't dig a hole in him, just knocked the hair off. And you know, that old horse sat down on his butt and started pawing her on the head and *knocked her out!* I thought he'd killed her. Her old eyes rolled back in her head. Self-defense was second nature to them old horses.

We had one cow with a white stripe down her shoulder. Somebody had cut a tendon in her knee so she couldn't run so fast. Some old cowboy had roped her and cut that tendon, thinking he could get her. So she was crippled.

The way we had to gather those cattle was to throw them into a thicket and then gather the thicket. And you couldn't see three feet in front of you, hardly. You could drive this old striped cow into the thicket, but getting her out was something else. She'd come running right at you in that thicket and you couldn't go anywhere. She always had eight or ten head with her, and I'm sure that most of them were her calves. They were all long-eared cattle—meaning they were unbranded mavericks.

Well, she'd gotten away from me the spring before, the same way. This time I heard or seen her coming, and I just blared it out of that thicket as fast as I could get out, and I had my rope down. I had me a loop built, and when she come out of there, I roped her and tripped her, and when she went down, she stuck one horn into the ground and couldn't get up.

She was old and poor and I didn't figure she'd make the winter, so I just got down and cut her throat. Later, I told the wagon boss about it and he said, "She's lived too long anyway."

We used different kinds of throws on wild cattle, depending on what they were. On bulls we roped half-heads. If you rope a bull by the horns, he'll stand out there at the end of the rope and toss his head around and wear your horse down so he can catch him and kill him. If you rope them by the neck, a lot of times you'll choke 'em to death because you can't get slack into the loop. But if you catch a half-head, you can give it slack.

From time to time, we would forefoot cattle. Coyote Morris taught me how to forefoot. Usually we forefooted just for the heck of it, or if we had one that ran off and wouldn't stay around the feed ground, we'd kind of roll that loop over his withers and head him back.

We crippled quite a few, forefooting. What happens is that you'll start out having both front feet, but by the time you turn off and take out the slack, the loop will be just on that outside foot. It breaks a lot of shoulders. I've quit using it.

The most success I had with those bunch-quitters was to build a little loop and drop it over his behind as I rode past, and then take a short dally. It turns them over and it sounds like it's breaking every bone in their body, but it's sure good for bunch-quitters.

I only weighed 130 pounds, but I could hold a sixteen-hundred– to seventeen-hundred–pound steer on the ground by myself. If you grab that top hind leg and just get a bear hug on it and roll back, he'll kick and shake you, but if he can't get that hind foot on the ground, he can't get up. They won't struggle but for a very short while and then they'll quit.

It takes patience, but you don't have much choice. You can't overpower a big old steer like that. You just have to wait until he goes along with it, until he runs out of want-to. They'll kick six or seven times and then they'll quit—for about ten seconds. And you can sure tie one or shackle him. You'd better, once you start.

I never turned my horse's head to one of those big cattle. You can't handle those big cattle, backing a horse up. While you were working on the ground, the horse would be grazing around. If they ever got a chance, they would leave you afoot. Most of those horses, all they wanted was to wait for a chance to kill you.

One time Berl Teague and I had followed some steers up near the head of Tule Creek. There were some great big old grapevines up there, as big around as your arm. We'd get into the middle of those things and the horses would get hung up and we'd have to saw our way out with a horn saw.

Them old steers went up on top and then they went back down into the canyon, and we were after them. Teague rode an old horse named Ranicky Bill, and he'd stub his toe every fifty yards. Nobody wanted to ride him, even though he was a good horse. Berl had shod him, had four new shoes on him.

He was in front of me, and here they went off. I was riding what I considered a pretty good horse. He could stand up. I'd had him over some pretty tough country. So I pulled his throttle out and down we went. When we got in that night, old Ranicky Bill had lost three of his shoes.

We came to a little fork in the trail. One of them steers went left and Teague went after him and I went after the others. One of them was a good ways behind the other and I was getting pretty close to him. He'd got down in this old creek bed and the sides of it must have been twelve feet high.

I seen the rocks falling off the side of the bank in front of me, and out of nowhere, and here come a little gray horse off of there, and the man who was riding him roped that steer.

It was Bobby Thompson, Tuffy Thompson's brother, and this was the first time I'd ever seen him. He must have been working for some outfit over on the south side of the canyon, or maybe his daddy had a place leased. He hadn't seen me, I guess.

That little old horse wouldn't have weighed 950 pounds. I got to visiting with him and he said, "This horse just come down the road one day. I know he belongs to somebody." He had never roped off of him, and he'd roped that big old steer. I'll bet he weighed fifteen hundred pounds.

I tell you what, that Bobby Thompson is a pretty good hand.

I'll tell you an amusing story about him. When he was a boy, his daddy was a heavy equipment operator. Bobby was a kid who would rope anything, everything. His daddy had just finished building a big tank dam and he was smoothing up the top.

Bobby sneaked up there and roped his right brake lever and jerked that dozer over the side of the dam. Messed up his pretty job. Bobby said that got him into a world of trouble.

Working around those old wild cattle, we were always getting a horse hooked. By the time we'd catch one of those old cows in the brush, the horse would be give out and a little slow to get out of the way. They were always getting punched around and scabbed up. A lot of horses got hooked.

Those old cows knew the rough places in the brush. We'd go after them into the brush but we couldn't get a loop on them. Finally we'd hit a little opening and they'd turn around and go to fighting. Your horse would be wore out, but your first thought was to go ahead and catch the old things anyway, whether they were running or looking at you. It was our job to catch them, after all.

One time C. H. Long got involved in a bad deal. A bull came after his horse and C. H. whirled him to get out of the way. The bull's horn scraped the horse on the hind leg and the horse kicked at him. The bull went on and got his horn under the flank cinch, and he couldn't get it out again. They were hung up, the horse and the bull. The last I saw of them, they were going through those mesquites together. I guess they finally got a-loose.

I saw Boots O'Neil get scratched up by one. At that time I'll bet Boots didn't weigh more than 110 pounds. He was a little-bitty guy when he come out there. He was fifteen or sixteen years old but he was little. His stirrups came down about halfway on those big old horses' sides. We had to help him on some of those horses; he just couldn't get on some of them. He was on a bronc, pretty green, and he roped this big old steer, caught him too deep around the belly. He fed out too much slack in his loop. I've done the same thing many times. You ride up on one of those big old things and you think, "This loop ain't going to be big enough," so you feed it another coil. And that's

39

what he did. He caught the steer around the belly and they went on opposite sides of a tree. The steer came up with the long end of the rope, and he started punching around on that old bronc with his horns. Boots hollered for help. We couldn't get to him. There was a big wash—we called them "guts"—between us and there was no way to get across it. I rode up to where I could see him, and he said, "Come here and bring somebody with you!" Somebody else had heard him hollering, and we finally got over there to him.

He had that steer tied down and was sitting on him! Had his neckerchief off and his coat off, and that old bronc was standing nearby, skinned up pretty good.

I said, "How in the world did you get that steer down?"

He said, "That rope slipped down around his flanks and he laid down."

In 1948, I had this JA horse we called No Can Sabe. He was a dun horse. When he got hot, he'd lock up and wouldn't move. He'd *sull.*

One day I roped a cow. We weren't supposed to be roping those cows without a reason, but this was a "training deal." I thought the horse needed to be roped on and I did it.

I roped this cow and she had a good set of horns on her, maybe a foot long on each side. No Can Sabe pulled one of those sulling deals, and that cow stuck her horn in him right behind the flank cinch. I was looking down at it, and she ran her horn into his belly plumb up to her head.

Of course he kind of unsulled then and we broke a-loose from her. I rode him back to the wagon and told Bud Long what had happened. He went and got that old 62 Smear that we put on fresh wounds to keep the flies away. He took that dope swab and told me to get a hold on the horse's ear, and he jobbed that thing up in him as far as he could get it and turned him out.

I figured he'd die, but in three months I went back to riding him. I don't know how the horn missed hitting something vital in there.

That experience sure changed his attitude about sulling. After that, when an old cow came ahooking out of the herd, you didn't want to be thinking about the girl you saw Saturday night.

Something similar happened to Tom Blasingame. He was riding a horse called Tom Thumb, the nicest little horse you ever saw. I believe he might have been one of the first King George horses out of that King Ranch stud. I don't remember what his year brand was, but I know that Tom did love that horse.

A man named Gene Harrison roped a bull and Blass rode in to heel it. The bull whirled to hook Tom's horse, and he broke Gene Harrison's rope. We didn't have nylon ropes back then, just had those old seven-sixteenths–inch grass ropes and they would break.

Well, that bull cut the honda out of Gene's rope and stuck a horn in Tom Thumb and just gutted him. He was trying to get away from the bull and his guts were falling out on the ground and got tangled up in his legs. He was kicking at his own guts, and the harder he kicked, the worse it got.

Tom Blasingame was really tore up about that. He thought the horse was dead, pulled off his saddle and left him there. The next morning he went out to feed his horses and he heard a horse nicker. He thought all the horses had come in, so he went down to check.

He went down to the horse pasture gate and there that little horse was, with his guts wrapped around his hind legs. He'd come home. And then Tom had to kill him. There wasn't anything else he could do.

Those were the Good Old Days, weren't they? Mmmm!

Glenn Green, Flower, and Other Broncs

In 1954, when I got out of the army, I went to work on the Smith ranch, northwest of Childress. They had a horse out there they called Piñata. When he was just a few days old, lightning killed his mother. The cowboys tried to find him but they didn't.

When they gathered all the mares out of that pasture in the fall, they still didn't find him, and they figured he was dead. The next spring they put the mares back in there, and in the fall they gathered them again, and he was with them. How he survived without his mother, I don't know. It was very unusual.

They put some old weekend cowboy to work breaking him, and by the time I got there, he had built up some bad habits and he wasn't popular.

I liked him. He was about as athletic a horse as you could ask for, but he thought pretty tough. He'd growed up tough. He hated a man. I guess he thought that everything that breathed was his enemy, except maybe another horse. There's no telling what all he had to deal with when he was a little feller.

His main lick was to whirl to the right when you tried to get on him. He wouldn't do anything when you put that left foot into the stirrup, but when that right foot left the ground . . . watch out! A lot of horses have different tricks they'll pull. Fortunately, this one did the same thing every time, and I figured out how to prepare for it. I'd take about three wraps of those bridle reins around my hand before I tried to get on. I thought he was a wonderful horse. You could just look at him and tell he was a good one. He'd look at you. Me and him kind of had a feeling for one another. I had to rope him to catch him, but I could go up to him and put the bridle on without any trouble. But if anybody else tried it, he was liable to get kicked.

He made a good using horse. I could do anything on him, but I had to remember his disposition. If I got down to tie a cow, I had to make sure that he couldn't leave me, because he would. He was a good cow horse, a fox-trotting son of a gun. He was a pleasure to ride, once you got on him. I'll tell you, the safest place to be around him was in the saddle.

Occasionally he tried to buck with me. He never did buck me off, but I knew that he could. He'd tell me what he was thinking about and I'd bump him and wool him around a little. The closest he ever came to bucking me off, I was going around the side of a hill when an airplane came over pretty low. I looked up at it and that sucker ducked off of that hill and went at it. That was the closest he ever got, and if he'd had two more jumps, he'd have done it then, but I had things pretty well under control and stopped it before everything went plumb to pieces.

I knew his habits and all, and how to deal with them, but that ranch changed hands and I left, and Piñata didn't have any friends out there anymore. Nobody could even get on him. They tied him to a tree and left him there without food or water for a week, and they still couldn't get on him. They sold him to the packers. I'd like to have known about it. I would have gone and got that little feller. I'll always have a warm place in my heart for him. That story about how he started off in life was enough to make me like him.

When I was working for Mendota Cattle Company in Roberts County, we had a horse on a place near Skellytown. The cowboys over there wouldn't ride him, and it was understandable why they wouldn't. I had never seen a horse with so many bad habits. Just about everything he did was wrong, now, and he was not going to accept discipline. He was an old gray Thoroughbred horse.

I'm sure that somebody had taken to getting him out of a stock trailer either with a pitchfork or a hotshot, and when you opened the gate, he'd got in the habit of coming out of there just as fast as he could, and whirling to the right. Then he'd be gone.

Them boys had to catch him three times in one morning and I was over there, and I said, "We're going to have to do something about that." You just couldn't have a horse doing that. I took him for the day and had another boy with me. I said to him, "If you tell what's fixing to happen, I'm gonna kill you. Not only will you be out of a job, you won't need one 'cause you'll be dead, because this may kill this horse."

We unloaded the other boy's horse and that left the gray horse in the front. I put my rope around his neck and laid the coils across the saddle horn where I could get to it. Then I told that boy to watch me so I didn't back off the bluff, and I backed the trailer up to a bluff that went right straight down about ten feet. Then I tied my catch rope to the back of the trailer, so that if he lived, I could catch him. And then I opened the gate.

And here he came out of there and went flying off that bluff. I thought it broke every bone in his body. But it didn't even hurt him. I went down and drove him out. You wouldn't want to try that trick on a horse you thought very much of, but with him I didn't think we had much to lose.

From then on, you had to go and get him out of that trailer. And he would try to kick the fire out of you. It was a bad old deal. If you just touched him, he'd kick. So one day I pulled him down there by the corral and got a water hose and turned it on him and let him kick until he got tired of it.

That same horse, when you were in caprocks, he wouldn't just climb, he'd go to lunging and you couldn't do a thing about it. Then he'd get to the top and whirl and jump back down wherever he could and maybe land on one leg, scare you to death. Finally I got to where I'd take down my rope and double about three foot of it, and when he hit the bottom I was ready to work it on him.

And you couldn't get on the son of a gun, had to take two wraps around your arm with the bridle reins. He'd just whirl and kick you. You couldn't catch him, had to rope him.

When I first started working with him, I'd grab him by the cheek of the bridle and kick him in the belly. And then to get on him, I used a trick I'd learned from Boyd Rogers. I took my left boot heel and started about his knee and stomped down that front leg until he went to picking it up.

44

After you've done that several times, when you pick your foot up, he'll pick *his* foot up, and you put your foot in the stirrup and get on him while his foot's up.

A horse can't think of but one thing at a time. And that's the way I got him to where I could get on him. And once I got on him, I just rode the fire out of him.

The old boy who had him was a good cowboy, but I think that horse had done something to him, made him scared. He'd hobble him to saddle him.

One morning, after I'd been working with the horse for a while, that boy was helping me. It was way before daylight and we were going to gather some heifers. I caught that old horse and led him up to the saddle house. He was standing there with me but it was so dark he couldn't see the horse. I led the horse up there and dropped the reins and throwed my saddle on him.

And he said, "By the way, what did you ever do with that old horse I used to ride?" I said, "Oh, he's around here somewhere."

When we got to the pasture it was daylight and he saw the horse, and he said, "Why you son of a gun, that's him!"

I had the utmost respect for Glenn Green. That man was a *cowboy*. I first ran into him when I was a kid. We was working a cattle drive over in New Mexico. Glenn and another man fell in on the drive. I was pretty green and I'd never heard fellows hoo-rah each other about their wives.

When we wound up at the roundup ground, I was between them. One of them said, "Hey, how's your wife and my kids?" The other one said, "Them kids are getting hungry, you'd better bring some groceries over." I thought they were a couple of toughs and there was fixing to be some bloodshed, so I took off and held the cuts.

I later found out that they *were* tough. They were working on a ranch over there in New Mexico and at night they'd go into town and clean out a whole bar. It got to where those bars didn't have any customers left. Everybody was afraid to go in them, and finally Glenn and this other old boy couldn't buy a beer in that whole country. Nobody would sell them one.

Well, years later Glenn had a rodeo string, and then moved to Higgins. A fellow named Brack LaGrone owned the cafe there and was trading horses, and Glenn went to work for him. And he helped Red Snyder for a long time. Everybody liked him.

Then he went to work for Barbys on the Beaver River. I think Red Snyder got him acquainted with Stanley Barby. Then he moved back to Higgins and ran the Packsaddle Bar, between Arnett, Oklahoma, and the Canadian River, and things went to going bad for him. Running a bar was the last thing he needed to do.

I've heard a lot of stories about Glenn. He was the nicest fellow in the world, but anybody who knew him didn't mess with him. I heard a story about Glenn when he was in Hereford. An old toughie come into a bar there and asked, "Who's the toughest guy here?" The bartender pointed to Glenn and said, "There he sits."

He went over to Glenn and said, "I understand you're tough."

And Glenn said, "No, I ain't tough. Go on. You got the wrong information."

That old boy kept fooling with him and picking at him, and Glenn said, "Now, I told you I ain't tough." But the old boy kept on, so Glenn got up and thrashed him. They said it took almost thirty seconds.

When it was over, the old boy said, "I thought you said you weren't tough."

And Glenn said, "I ain't, but if you want to meet some people who are, I'll introduce you. But I can tell you that you don't want to meet 'em."

Glenn never made ripples, never bothered anybody or caused anybody to have ill feelings towards him. But one of those wise guys . . .

He wasn't a very big storyteller until you kind of got him started. He wouldn't talk about himself. But he could come out of the clear blue with some of the dangedest off-the-wall expressions that would just knock you down. I think it was the shock of what he said. You weren't expecting to hear that particular phrase. Glenn Green sure made a lot of people happy. He made a few unhappy, but they sure was wiser for it.

One time at Higgins, a man took a horse to Glenn. He was like me, he worked with problem horses, and he suggested they bring the horse to me. This was a snuffy son of a gun, but that ain't why Glenn sent him to me.

Glenn was a better bronc rider than I was. He was just like a piece of petrified wood. Tough! A horse could kick him and cripple himself. He could ride anything he decided to. I heard of one deal he got into. Glenn didn't throw the towel in, but the old boy who owned the horse said, "I've got to go get that roan horse or him or Green is going to get killed. I think it's a toss-up who's going to die first."

Glenn and I had this system worked out. If I had a toughie, I'd send him to Glenn, and if he had one that needed a special touch, he sent him to me. It was a good system, especially for me.

This was a class horse, a black horse with four white legs, just a beautiful animal, and the bronckiest son of a gun you ever saw. He wasn't really mean but he'd gotten by with some things he shouldn't have.

I'd ridden him around the house a few times when a pipeline crew come though and left a gate down, and I had a bunch of cattle mixed up. I was going out there to straighten them up and took my wife. I cut off an old cow and took her off, shoved her out there, and that horse was watching the cow. I thought, "Boy, this horse is going to be all right."

I cut another cow off and they kind of split. One of them started to come back and I punched him out there, and say! He didn't go to bucking, he just started running and jumping, and every jump was higher than the one before. I knew he was going to fall. We hit some old washed out trails out there and down he went. So I just tied the little feller down and left him.

Usually when I tie a horse down, I'll tie a front foot to the saddle horn and they'll get mad and lay down. You have to tie their head around to the flank cinch or they'll beat it against the ground. You can't leave one's head loose.

I borrowed my wife's horse and left her at the pickup and went and finished my work. It took me about two hours, and when I come back to that pickup, I believe that was the maddest lady I ever saw.

Anyway, we went over there to where I'd left that horse tied down, and he nickered when he heard us coming. I said to my wife, "We have won this battle, sure as the world." And everything went good from then on.

Well, we consigned him to a sale in Clovis, New Mexico. He rang the bell over there. He was the highest-selling horse in the sale. And a fellow from Las Vegas, Nevada, bought him for his fourteen-year old daughter. I told this fellow who owned the horse, "You'd better tell him he don't need that horse for his girl." And he said he'd already told him, and the man had said that his daughter could ride him.

About two years after that, I was showing a cutting horse out in Lamar, Colorado, and playing fiddle at a rodeo dance, and I saw a girl riding that black horse. I asked her where she got him. She said, "My daddy traded four wore-out geldings for him. A friend of his bought him and his little girl couldn't ride him. She had a trainer and he couldn't ride him, so they swapped him off before he got any worse. Daddy traded for him and got him fixed, and this is the Utah barrel-horse champion."

So the next year, I was watching the National Finals Rodeo and that sucker won fourth in the barrel racing. But I really believe if he'd run as fast around those barrels as he did with me when he ran off, he'd have won first place.

In 1984 I went to work for Larry Dawson, on a ranch south of Arnett, Oklahoma. I was riding some young horses for him and doing some cowboy work. He told me there was a little paint horse there I didn't need to mess with. Benny Beutler had had him in his bucking string and gave him to Dan Pearson's boy to use as a practice bucking horse.

His name was Flower and somehow Dawson had ended up with him.

The foreman over there was Jim Lamb, and I'd pulled a prank or two on Jim. There were six paint horses there, and I asked Jim which one was the Benny Beutler horse. He pointed to one

48

of them, but he showed me the wrong one. He was aiming to get me bucked off, see.

I left the good horse alone and went to riding Flower. I noticed that he was kind of rough and he was bad about running into other horses. But I rode him for three or four months and finally got him kind of lined out. I wouldn't ride anything else for a week at a time. I'd already decided it was going to take some riding to get him going in the right direction.

One day old Larry come in and saw me on him, and he said, "What are you doing on that ignorant thing? I told you not to fool with him." About then, Jim Lamb got down in the middle of that corral, he was laughing so hard, and we all figured out what had happened.

About that time I sold one of my good horses, a dun called Jake, and I told Larry I wanted to buy Flower from him. He said, "If you'll get him off this place, you can have him."

About that time, this job on the Gray ranch opened up and I got it. I was out one day showing the ranch to my new bosses, Keith and Roger Gray. I knew there was a bad spot in the fence, so I trotted over there to look at it. It was in a little canyon over there.

As I was going down the hill, Flower looked back at the other horses and I punched him. He kept looking, so I jobbed him with both spurs, and say, that was sure a mistake. He bucked me off, pretty easily. Roger and Keith didn't see it, I was glad of that

Later on, I was working Flower in the pasture and instead of turning back with the cow, Flower would run on past her. He'd watch a cow real good to the left but not to the right. He'd run on past one and I couldn't turn him. He wouldn't respond.

So I got a short rope, about twenty feet long, and put the horn loop around his neck and found me about an eight-hundred–pound steer in a water lot. I trotted Flower down the fence after him. When the steer stopped, Flower went on, so I just pitched my loop on that steer.

And say, it did wreck things. He kept going, as I knew he would. When the slack went out of the rope, it jerked him around and sent me rolling.

49

I got back on him and ran that yearling down a fence again, side by side. Directly Flower ran past him again. The yearling stopped and turned behind us, and Flower got another jerk. By the third time, I was getting pretty gun-shy. I thought this might not be as good an idea as I'd thought, or I might not live long enough to find out if it was.

But the third time the yearling tried to go behind us, I saw Flower's ear go down. He was watching. It gave him a hard jerk but he stayed on his feet. I decided I'd do it one more time.

I really built a fire under him this time and he didn't even look when the steer turned back. I roped the steer and it was a terrible deal. It throwed me off out there and kind of knocked the air out of me. I got to crawling around and looked and saw that both of them were choking down.

Flower had backed out to the end of the rope. His eyes were sticking out and he was choking. The steer was choking. I couldn't cut the rope on the horse's end. If you even touched him, he'd go to jumping and carrying on. You could hear him breathing for half a mile. The steer fell down, so I ran over and cut the honda out of my rope and got it off him.

Then I had to get the horn loop off of Flower. I got a little slack in the rope, enough to give him some air, but it was still hung. Every time I touched him, he'd throw a fit. Getting it off of him was almost as bad as getting jerked down. I finally got a hold on him and got him eared down and took the rope loose.

I sat there for a while, smoked a cigarette, got back on that little feller and trotted the steer back down that fence, and, say, he *did* turn around when the steer did.

I've still got the horse and he gets a little better all the time. I've roped calves on him out in the pasture. The little scamp is fast and he's a good draggin' horse. He's pretty stout, and he gets stouter when you go to peckin' on him with the spurs. He's not as good a horse as some people ride, and he's not as good a horse as some of the ones I've got, but knowing what he used to be, I feel pretty good about him.

Danny Boy and Easy Does It

I'm a firm believer in riding good horses. I've had three crackerjack horses in my life, which is two more than most people ever have.

That kind doesn't just happen. You have to spend extra time on them. On an average horse, you might spend extra time because you have to. Them good ones, you spend the extra time because you want to.

Danny Boy may have been the best horse I ever threw a leg over. He wasn't supposed to happen. The stud got out and bred the mare, and the colt belonged to a lady there in Memphis, Texas. I was playing fiddle with Bob Wills at the time and I was in Memphis one day and saw the colt. I knew his momma and daddy because I had broke both of them to ride. The colt looked just like that old stud.

His mother was out of a Thoroughbred mare by Flying Bob. I can't remember what her mother's name was. She was by an old horse named Excite and the stud was a remount horse. They were known to be broncky. His daddy was a straight Thoroughbred horse named Freckles, by Wild Tent, and Wild Tent won the polo pony sire class four years in a row in London. He throwed good colts.

First chance I got, I stopped in to see that lady. I already had two children then, and she said, "Frankie, if you'll come home and raise those children and quit running all over the world playing that fiddle, I'll give you that little colt."

I waited until he got to be a two-year-old and I come home. She gave him to me and I brought him up here to Lipscomb County. He was athletic, he could do things, and he understood me. I could do things with him the first time and he picked them up.

Just for instance, one time I had to load a dead calf into the back of the pickup. He kept hanging up on the tail gate. I took

51

my rope and ran it over the top of the headache rack and went back to the tail end. I'd tell Danny Boy to go and he'd take one step. I'd tell him again and he'd take another step.

We understood each other. He would tell me things. There are things a horse will tell you and you'd better listen. He let me know that the day was coming when he'd buck me off, and sure enough, he did.

I knew it was coming but he kind of caught me in a weak moment. He slipped down on a terrace, and when he got up I was off in left field. He bucked me off pretty good, and then he kept on trying it. But he'd tell me it was coming and I could beat him to the punch. He wasn't a cheatin' son of a gun. He'd warn you, and he never bucked me off again.

The first tragedy involving Danny Boy came when I had to sell him and load him up. I sold him to a diamond merchant from New York, and I'll tell you, I had water in my eyes when I loaded him up.

The next tragedy came when I found out he'd burned to death in a barn. It was a big fire that burned a hundred head of polo ponies.

I wished I hadn't found that out.

In 1979 I was working for J. D. Barton in Lipscomb County. A feller called me up and asked if I could ride a horse for him. I'll call him Easy Does It, although that wasn't his real name. He was out of Easy Jet. I was taking care of twenty-two sections of ranch country, and I said, "I can't, unless he's already broke. I can't afford to get crippled."

He said, "Well, my fifteen-year-old boy can ride him. He just needs to look at a cow." I told him to bring him on.

About a week later, after we'd delivered our cattle, he brought the horse. The first time I looked at his head, I *knew* what I was looking at. I didn't ride him for a while. About two o'clock one day I got on him. I had an uneasy feeling about him so I told Spud Hawkins, "You need to come with me in case something happens." And something did happen.

I'd been leading him on horseback because I knew I hadn't heard all the story on him yet. I got on him and was riding him around in the corral, and he just blew up with me. He was pitching hard. He was powerful. Those Easy Jets are athletes. He just blowed me away. I knew I was bucked off by the second jump. I throwed my reins away because I wanted to get away from him. He was kicking as high as a barn. I put my hands on the fork of the saddle and shoved myself away from him, and just as I pushed, he kicked. The cantle of the saddle slapped me on the butt and drove me way up in the air.

There was an eight-foot water tank in the corner of that pen, and it didn't look any bigger than a dime. I had a lot of time to think because I was way up there, and I thought, "Frankie, you've lucked out a lot of times, but son, this time something bad's going to happen." It did. I hit on my shoulder. The ground in those pens had been beat down by cattle and horses and it was as hard as rock. It tore my shoulder all a-loose. My arm was hanging five inches beyond where it should have.

I'd just got to the house and was fixing to call the doctor in Shattuck, and the owner of the horse called. I was hurting pretty bad. He asked how I was getting along with that horse. I said, "Let me tell you something about that fifteen-year-old boy of yours. He's got a pretty good future ahead of him if he can ride that crazy son of a gun."

He said, "I was afraid of that."

I told him to come get the horse. I couldn't ride him and didn't want him on the place.

I knew my shoulder was messed up, but what we didn't know was that it had busted my lung. It wasn't an explosive thing. One lung had a little hole in it and it was seeping air. All the air went out of it and filled my chest cavity and stopped the other lung from working.

It liked to have got me. I thought I was dying. I knew everything that was going on around me but I couldn't do anything, couldn't talk or breathe. When the doctor got there, he put one of those trocars into the collapsed lung and went to putting air into it. As soon as he got some air in it, it went to

53

working, but the other one didn't because there was so much pressure against it.

That was about as close to being dead as I ever was, or that I knew about.

They had to get that lung fixed before they could give me anesthetic to fix my shoulder. They had to put two pins in it. I was in the hospital for something like two weeks.

When I come home, I had my arm in a sling. Two days later, I had a load of calves come in. Couple of days later, I got another load. I learned how to take my arm out of the sling, and I could carry feed sacks and pull windmills. It didn't hurt as long as I kept it against my side. I didn't miss a day's work with it, once I got home.

I couldn't saddle a horse and I couldn't get anybody else to do it for me. They didn't think I ought to be riding. If I found a sure 'nuff sick calf, I had friends who would come over and get him in. But then I found one in the pasture that was sick, and I knew I didn't have time to call anyone. This calf was bad sick. I don't know why I hadn't seen him sooner and kept him up. I hooked the trailer onto my pickup and went in and asked my wife to saddle a horse for me. She said she wasn't going to do it. I said, "Well, I can and I'm going to, some way. I'll figure out a way to do it, so you just as well help me."

She did and I loaded a horse in the trailer and went out in the pasture. I got on my horse and found the calf and got pretty close to him. I hit him right behind the head on the first loop and missed, but on the next one, I stuck it on him. I had thought it might hurt my shoulder, but it didn't.

But when I drug him up to the trailer, I had to raise my arm to throw the rope over the racks, and oh! That was painful. When the doctor took out those pins, one of them was bent, and that's probably when I bent it.

Even to this day, that shoulder is very tender. I can't carry a sack of feed on it and it's got a hump on it.

I later found out that the man who'd called me couldn't get anybody to ride that horse. He had a bad reputation, and my friends told me, "If I'd known you were going to ride that son of a gun, I'd have told you to leave him alone."

Easy Does It worked on my mind. No cowboy wants to say that he's afraid of a horse, so we use the term "respect." He'd taught me to respect a horse a lot more than I did before. What it boils down to is that he'd made me afraid of those tough horses. I didn't want that to happen to me again because I want to play the fiddle. When I get to where I can't play the fiddle and just start taking up space on this earth, I may go back to riding those crazy things.

Frankie's Waltz

I remember the best of the cowboys
All said that you rode like you played,
That you tuned your horse like your fiddle
With the best pair of hands ever made.
As we all gather round in the evenin'
At the end of another long day,
I still remember the feelin'
When I heard some old cowboy say—
Frankie, take out your fiddle.
Would you rosin your bow?
Would you play me an old waltz or two that you know?
With your heart on your shoulder, up under your chin,
Would you play "Spanish Eyes" or "Westphalia" again?

Words and music by E. H. Crossland

2

Cowboy Fiddler
in Bob Wills's Band

There are more fiddle players in hell than any other kind
of people.

Memphis, Texas, preacher

If there was somebody I wanted to get even with, I'd give
him a fiddle and three lessons.

Growing Up in Bob Wills Country

My family lived in Hall County, Texas, not far from where Bob Wills grew up, and they all knew Bob and had gone to his dances before he went to Ft. Worth and made a name for himself. He lived at Turkey and played at Lakeview and Memphis. We lived near a little old place called Plaska.

I started school at Plaska. I got five whippings the first day, I'll never forget that. This old kid sitting behind me stuck me with a sharp pencil, and I just turned around and bloodied his nose. The rest of the whippings were for talking when I wasn't supposed to and going to the bathroom without asking. I thought if you needed to go, that was your business.

I grew up in a musical home. My mother's people were very musical. They came from Alabama. My grandfather's name was I. J. Tucker. He had a big family and was an evangelist. He played the organ and he would compose songs and sell 'em for fifty dollars apiece. He sold 'em to a publishing company. He wrote "Wait for the Wagon," "Be My Life's Companion and You'll Never Grow Old," and "Let a Smile Be Your Umbrella on a Rainy Day." The Mills Brothers later recorded "Be My Life's Companion."

All of my mother's family could sing and their father had taught them harmony. When they'd get together, maybe they hadn't seen each other for twenty years but they'd hit one of them old tunes and it sounded like they'd practiced it the night before. They had sung together as little girls and each one knew her part.

My uncle was the Alabama fiddle champion for so many years, they got to where they wouldn't let him play in the contest. He just missed being the world champion a couple of times.

He'd come to Texas occasionally and play for us. His son played the guitar, played the fire out of the guitar. I've seen that old man stop and kick him on the shins for playing the wrong chord. He'd say, "Don't play that, I told you that was wrong!"

My father was a cotton farmer and could hardly even play the radio, but he could dance. He loved to dance, and he was so proud of me when I learned to play the fiddle. He thought Bob Wills was the greatest thing he'd ever known. Mother loved to dance too. She is seventy-nine years old and living in Hall County, and she still goes to four dances a week.

I was aware of Bob Wills for as long as I can remember. He had quite an impact on that country. We used to hear him on the radio. With them old weak batteries in the radios, people wouldn't even turn them on until Saturday night, when Bob Wills come on, and Mother and Daddy both had their ears to the radio and if we scooted a chair, it was sure the wrong thing to do.

While Bob was in Ft. Worth playing with the Light Crust Dough Boys, he was getting quite famous. He loved people and he loved crowds, but he'd get tired of them. He'd get to longing for his old home people. He'd escape from Ft. Worth and come back to Hall County. I remember one time, everybody was excited. I wasn't very old, hadn't started school yet. Bob Wills was home and was going to play a dance at one of those farm houses over on the Red River. This old guitar player named Zip Durris played with him. He still lives in the same place he did then.

My folks took me down there. I didn't get to meet Bob. They shut us kids up in a room by ourselves—well, not by ourselves. There was the meanest old woman in there with us you ever saw. I could hear that fiddle and I wanted to see Bob Wills playing it, and I'd start in there and she'd get me by the ear and set me on the bed. It was miserable.

That was my first association with Bob Wills.

Long before I met Bob Wills, I'd been mentally involved with him. After I started playing the fiddle, playing with him was my ambition. When I was working on the JA ranch and learning to play the fiddle around the wagon at night, those old cowboys would make fun of me because I couldn't play very well. I'd tell them, "One of these days I'm going to play for Bob Wills and y'all are going to be sorry that you laughed."

Of course, I just said that. I never dreamed of getting to do it.

When I quit the JA, I went to work for Jack Molesworth, south of Clarendon, out by Lelia Lake, actually, where Ace Reid was born. This would have been the winter of '49. We got snowed in that winter and couldn't go anywhere. They had a piano and I got to fooling with it. His wife was from England and was a schooled piano player. She could play the fire out of that piano, and she told me, "You need to take some lessons." I didn't think much about it. I could play anything I wanted to with one hand.

By the way, while I was working for Molesworths that winter, the windmill broke down and we were low on water. It was Saturday and we were going to town. I lived in the bunkhouse with this kid named Fred, the worst kid I'd ever seen. Me and Fred were going to take a bath up at the big house, and Fred told me, "Frankie, we're going to have to use the same tub of water."

I said, "I don't care, go ahead."

Fred put a bunch of soap in that bath water, so I couldn't see the bottom. I stuck my foot in there and touched a piece of metal. It was the chain of a wolf trap! He'd set that wolf trap right where I would have sat down.

When I left there, I went to work for Billy Lewis on the RO ranch. We were down at the Ox Bow Camp one day and there was an old boy down there who had a fiddle. It rained us out and we were sitting around that bunkhouse and I got to fooling with the fiddle. I could pick out about anything on it.

Billy Lewis was trying to take a nap. I think he'd been partying the night before. After a while he raised up and said, "Why don't you let that little feller rest." So I put the fiddle away and didn't fool with it any more.

Some time later, we were shipping cattle over at Romero, near Channing. We went into the cafe to eat dinner and "Faded Love" was the only thing that played on the jukebox the whole time we were there. Just as soon as it ended, they played it again. And I thought that was the most beautiful thing I'd ever heard in my life.

I asked someone, "What is it that's making that racket we like?" And he said, "That's Bob Wills's fiddle." And I said, "You know, I believe I'll just buy me one and learn to play that song. I don't care if I learn anything else, but I'm going to learn that one song."

I loved the sound Bob got out of a fiddle, that old lazy, creepy sound he had. It sounded lonesome to me, Bob's playing did. I learned to play a lot of other stuff but my love was Bob Wills's fiddle.

All musicians go through stages. I wanted to play jazz at one time and I had some pretty good teachers, but I saw that it didn't have the impact on the people that the plain old vanilla songs did. I could touch people with it, and I got to looking around and it dawned on me that they were the ones paying those dollars.

I decided to play for them, not for other musicians.

The Cowboy's First Fiddle

In November of 1950 I quit the Lewis ranch and was going down the street in Memphis, Texas. There was a hock shop there, and a fiddle was sitting in the window. Twenty-seven dollars. I went in and bought it with my cowboy wages.

By the time I got home, the folks were already in bed and I got to fooling with that thing. I squawked and scraped on it all night.

The next morning I told Daddy I'd bought me a fiddle. He said, "The heck you did. I thought we either needed to grease that windmill or there was a hog hung under the gate."

I went to work breaking horses for Boyd Rogers, there at Memphis, and he could play the fiddle. Me and them old Thoroughbred colts would get into a war and Mr. Rogers would say, "Ah ah, just tie him up over there and let's go to the house and play the fiddle. He ain't going to learn anything and he ain't doing you no good either. You're both mad. It's all right if one of you is mad, but when both of you get mad, we need to tie him up."

The next spring when the JA wagon pulled out, I was with it. The old wagon boss on the JA, Bud Long, was a great whistler. He could whistle anything, and he'd put those little grace notes in there. He knew a lot of those old breakdown fiddle tunes. Around the wagon at night, he'd whistle a song and I'd try to play it. I'm sure that was pretty entertaining to the other cowboys 'cause I was having quite a bit of trouble with it.

I didn't know there was such a thing as a half-tone on a fiddle. Bud was trying to teach me "Ten Pretty Girls," and when he got to the bridge where it goes to that half-tone and seventh note, he'd whistle it and I'd say, "It ain't here."

And he'd say, "It's there. Now, you'd better get her this time 'cause I'm a-losing my pucker."

I never could find that note and I couldn't play that song for years and years. My band would get requests for it but I'd tell them that we didn't know it.

Then just a few years ago I was over at Miami, Texas, at a party and they were playing a record that had "Ten Pretty Girls" on it. I happened to have my fiddle behind the seat of my pickup and I just killed that party, went back and started the record over and learned that song.

In 1985 I was over in Silverton and I knew that Bud Long was living there, so I went over to his house and played that song for him. He said, "Frankie, I can see that I've accomplished at least one thing in my life. I've taught you how to play that song on the fiddle."

Bud Long had quite an impact on my playing. He wouldn't settle for just pretty good. He wanted me to do it right. It has paid off for me.

There was another old boy on the JA's, name was Jack Curry. I was just learning vibrato on the fiddle, and Jack would hear it and he'd say, "Why do you want to quiver that note?" I don't think he liked any note, but he liked a plain note better than one with vibrato.

I would sit around and practice my vibrato with one finger, but then I got a mesquite thorn stuck in it and it got as big as your thumb. I couldn't do the vibrato any more and he said, "I like that better."

I was a pretty good roper. You could nearly bet that I'd catch one, and I could catch them by the horns, half-head, or neck. Jack and I were out one time and jumped eight or nine wild cattle out of some cedars, and he said, "You know, I used to know an old kid who could sure rope, but then he started playing the fiddle and he got to where he couldn't catch a thing. That fiddle just ruined him."

We jumped those cattle and here we went, wide open. I said, "I want that one," and he said, "Don't forget what I said about that fiddle." I rode up and missed that cow a foot and a half, just hit her left horn a little and bounced off like a widow woman's loop.

And I didn't catch anything for three months! It did something to me, and Jack knew it. He said, "It's that fiddle, Frankie, I'm telling you, you need to quit playing it."

One night a bunch of us were sitting around the JA wagon. We had pulled two bedrolls together. I had a fiddle and another boy had his guitar, and I was tuning my fiddle. Them old pegs would get dry and you'd have to really bear down on them to get them to turn. I didn't know enough then to back them up first, instead of putting a lot of oomph on them.

I twisted too hard on the E string. It broke and hit that old guitar player on the nose and went through the skin. I mean, it stuck into his nose. He had quite a bit to say about that

In 1952 I was back to breaking horses for Boyd Rogers at Memphis. I remember when I was trying to learn to play "Right or Wrong" on his wife's old wind-up record player. It was on one of them old 78-rpm records with a purple label. I'd wind up that old record player and go to playing, but towards the end the record player had run down and I'd be out of tune with the song. It sounded like nine Egyptian fiddle students playing.

Mr. Rogers was an exceptional man, very intelligent and well read. He taught me a lot of what I know about horses and he encouraged me to play the fiddle. He played some, but he was a big, burly man and his fingers were as thick as sausages. Each one would cover about three strings. But he knew the notes and chords, and he encouraged me to play.

He could see that I was making progress. What I played might not be polished, but I could sit down and take a little time and play almost anything, if I knew the tune well.

When he realized that I was going to do something with my fiddle, he wanted me to take better care of my hands and quit digging postholes. He said that was something anyone could do and it would stiffen up my fingers. The day he decided that, he never let me get on another horse he thought could buck me off. He'd go get an old kid there in town and let him ride.

It hurt my pride. That old kid would go around town telling people that Frankie was getting scared of those horses.

While I was working on Mr. Rogers's ranch, I started playing at dances in Amarillo. The ranch was six miles north of Memphis. On the day I was going to play in Amarillo, I'd pick me out an old hateful bronc and lope him into Memphis. I had one fiddle at the ranch and another one in town. Mr. Rogers had helped me get the second fiddle. I couldn't carry a fiddle on a bronc, see.

When I got into Memphis, I'd tie my bronc to a tree, go to the house and get my fiddle, and catch a bus to Amarillo. A fellow named Curtis Marchbanks would pick me up at the bus station and we'd go play a dance. When it was over, he'd pay me my $13 and take me back to the bus station and I'd have to wait four hours to catch the next bus back to Memphis.

I'd get into Memphis about six in the morning, take my fiddle back to Mrs. Rogers's house, get back on that old bronc, and ride him out to the ranch. I'd lie down and get what usually seemed to me about ten minutes' sleep, and then Mr. Rogers would be knocking on the door,

"Hey! Got breakfast ready. You'd better get up."

I was drafted in the Army in '52. I'd been playing in a little band there at Samnorwood, Texas, between Shamrock and Memphis. Roger Miller took my place in that band. He'd grown up in Erick, Oklahoma, not too far from there, and he was a young blade then, learning to play the fiddle. This same old gentleman named Jack Prichard had helped both of us.

Roger replaced me as the fiddle player. He played pretty well. He was always coming up with some idiotic saying. That's been part of Roger Miller forever, the strange things he says.

I saw him on the Tonight Show one time, and I believe it was the best lick I ever saw Roger hit. Roy Clark was hosting the show and Roger was a guest. Roy had just bought this new high-dollar fiddle and was real proud of it.

Roy said, "Roger, why don't you come over here and look at my new fiddle." So Roger looked it over and said, "Roy, that's nice. Did you make it yourself?"

The next time I saw Roger, I was playing with the Miller Brothers Band and he was playing drums for Faron Young. We were playing a dance on a Thursday night in Wichita Falls and they were coming through and they stopped.

Roger come in and heard those three fiddles, and he said, "I want to play a tune or two." I said sure, and he played with us. Later that evening, he told me that he'd had eleven tunes in the Top Ten that year. Those were songs he'd written.

I haven't seen him since then, and probably never will. He's in New York now and I sure ain't going up there.

When I was drafted into the army, I took my fiddle with me. I was in Special Service about all the time. They sent me to Germany after basic training at Ft. Knox, Kentucky, and I played for the officers and enlisted men. I didn't know more than twenty songs.

I worked mainly as a comedian in the Special Services, not as a fiddle player. I'd tell two or three jokes and play the fiddle.

There's one time I'll never forget. We went to Vienna, Austria, and played in the opera house. I guess they'd never heard a breakdown fiddle. I got a twenty-minute ovation. I'd come out and take a bow. I never thought much about it except that it was holding up the show. They never whistled or anything, just clapped for twenty minutes.

That may have been my greatest moment, but I wasn't smart enough to know it.

When I got out of the army in 1954, I went back to work breaking horses for Boyd Rogers at Memphis. One Sunday, they brought Eck Robertson over from Amarillo to play at a function they were having.

Eck was a well-known fiddle player. By the time I knew him, he lived in Amarillo. He was the world champion fiddle player at the age of thirteen, and I don't know how many times he won it after that.

He and Bob Wills's family were well acquainted. They battled at those fiddlers' contests all the time, especially he and Uncle John Wills, Bob's daddy. One time Eck would win and the next time Uncle John would win. At one contest they played this tune called "Lost Indian" where they yelled in it. Uncle John beat him this time and Eck told somebody, "He didn't out-fiddle me, he out-hollered me."

Eck was pretty hard-nosed about it. He would get very resentful when he'd get beat, but then, he wasn't used to it. He probably won more fiddlers' contests in his life than any other fiddle player that's ever lived.

I don't know that he ever played against Bob in a contest. Bob never was too good at fiddlers' contests. He played his own type of music and that wasn't what won at the contests. But Bob was aware of Eck and Eck was aware of Bob. Bob told Doc Townsend that Eck got that "Brown Skinned Gal" from him, and Eck told me that *he* wrote it and that Bob got it from him.

One time, years later when I was playing with Bob Wills, we were at The Golden Nugget in Las Vegas. I played "Sally Gooden," and when we finished the show and were going back to the dressing room, Bob said, "I just wish Eck Robertson could have heard that."

A lot of people didn't like Eck. He was pretty cocky. Bob Wills used to say, "He's awfully sure of himself." Eck wrote a lot of tunes that a lot of folks aren't aware of. One of them he taught me and I've lost it, I can't remember how it goes, but I'll bet some of these fiddle players can do it. It was called "The Kansas City Rag." And he wrote "Brown Skinned Gal" and a tune he called "Raggedy Ann" which was later called "Ragtime Annie."

He wrote one called "The Amarillo Waltz," which is a beautiful thing and very, very difficult to play. He told me, "I've won more fiddlers' contests with that waltz than I have playing 'Sally Johnson.'"

But anyway, Mr. Rogers brought Eck Robertson over to Memphis to play at a Sunday deal. He was getting up in years by then and it wasn't long until he quit going to fiddlers' contests. He was getting real bad arthritis. He never ate right, never rested, people were always wanting him to come play for them. He'd go play just for his dinner. He'd be playing on stage and his hands would lock up on him and he'd drop his fiddle.

It would go clattering across the stage, just made you sick to see it.

He began to tie a string to his fiddle and put it around his neck so that if he dropped the fiddle, it wouldn't hit the floor.

But while he was there at the Rogerses' house in Memphis, Mr. Rogers asked him to listen to me play. By then, I was beginning to take a hold of the fiddle and Eck taught me a song called "Done Gone," which he wrote. He said, "Son, play my fiddle on that tune." I did, and it was real easy to play it on his fiddle. He said, "You know, that fiddle kind of fits you. When I don't need it any more, I'd kind of like for you to have it. You're going to make a fiddle player if you want to."

Now, this fiddle I'm referring to was one of two Eck carried with him. He had one tuned in A and he used it for playing "Sally Gooden," "Tom and Jerry," "Lost Indian," and all the tunes in A. If he was playing "Billy in the Low Ground" or "Sally Johnson" or something in another key, he'd play this fiddle I played.

One day sometime later, I came in from work. Mr. and Mrs. Rogers had gone somewhere and the house was empty. I wanted to play my fiddle but I couldn't find it. It wasn't where I left it. I looked all over the house and still couldn't find it. I was sick! I thought somebody had stole it. I moped around there all day, wondering how I could ever scrape up enough money to buy me another fiddle.

When Mr. Rogers came back that evening, I found out that he'd taken my fiddle to Amarillo and he'd brought back that fiddle of Eck Robertson's. I never knew how much money had changed hands on the deal, but I know that I broke a lot of horses that summer for three dollars a day.

Later on, I beat Eck in a contest at Shamrock, Texas, and he said, "I knew they were going to give it to you, but you didn't win that contest." I said, "Well, I sure agree with you, Uncle Eck." It made him madder than heck and he didn't have much to do with me after that.

Roping Rabbits and Fiddling Around

In 1956 I went to Bob Wills and asked him for a job. He was at the Clover Club in Amarillo, and I had been playing around with some bands.

He knew about me. I'd worked down in Waco with a feller named Leon Rausch who later worked with Bob, and is now one of the reknowned Texas Playboys, and to my way of thinking one of the greatest singers Bob Wills ever had—maybe *the* best.

I worked with him in a little old band down in Waco after I got out of the army, maybe '55 or '56. Then I quit and went back to Memphis and was training polo ponies for Boyd Rogers.

And Boyd told me, "Frankie, you need to go talk to Bob Wills about a job. Y'all have got the same feeling. Y'all could play such pretty fiddles together. It would be just like Bob playing two fiddles because you learned from his records, how to express a note."

So I went to Amarillo and asked Bob about a job. At that time he was the only fiddle player.

He said, "Naw son, things is tough. I'd like to have a hundred fiddles but I just can't afford one right now. What was your name again?"

Then I was playing out in Kermit, Texas, with a little old four-piece band, starving to death, playing old beer joints for eight dollars a night. And who appears in there but Leon Rausch. He came in that beer joint and said, "When are you going to take intermission?"

I said, "*Right now.*"

He said, "There's a feller out here I think you'd like to visit with."

We went out there and it was Bob Wills in the car. He said, "I've been listening to you out here for an hour, boy. I couldn't go in there because all these people know who I am and I wouldn't have been able to enjoy it. I sure like what I've been hearing.

People have been telling me about you and I thought we needed to come listen to you."

I thanked him, and then he said they had to be going. They were playing in Hobbs, New Mexico.

He said, "You're Frankie McWhorter, aren't you? I remember talking to you up at the Clover Club in Amarillo."

I never saw any more of him for a while.

In 1957 I was in Memphis, Texas, breaking horses on my own. After a while I began to notice that most of my business was coming from Childress, Texas, so I moved down there and went to work.

I was keeping my horses out at the sale barn and helping out at the sale every Wednesday. I'd push cattle to them on sale day and they'd pay me more than I was making breaking horses, the reason being that nobody paid me.

I was riding them horses and day-working some besides that. When I got one doing well enough, I'd take him and go help someone gather cattle, and while I was gone, people would come and pick up their horses. Without paying me. While I was in Childress, I heard that the Miller Brothers Band was looking for a fiddle player. I listened to them on the radio every day at twelve o'clock and I thought, boy, they played some nice, tough arrangements. They were a well-rehearsed group. And that's kind of what I had in mind to be a part of.

I went down to Wichita Falls and talked to them. They had just finished doing a radio show and I told them I'd heard they were looking for a fiddle player. They asked me to play a song and I played my interpretation of it. They said, "You're hired." They didn't even ask if I could play some of that hard stuff they did.

They asked me when I could go to work and I said, "Well, I've got a pen full of broncs back in Childress that I have to do something with." And besides that, we had planned this jack-rabbit roping contest. We already had the plans drawed up. Everybody was going to get rich on the deal.

Somebody had come up with the idea of having a jackrabbit roping and he'd asked me to help him. He'd said, "We'll cut you in on the profits." I thought that sounded like a winner. *Anybody* would come to a jackrabbit roping, just to see what it was. So we advertised it on the radio, had posters made, did some publicity.

The way we got these rabbits, we cut the bead out of a tractor tire and wove some fishing cord across it and made a kind of a net thing. It took five men to catch one rabbit. We'd go out at night to that old air base at Childress and there was a world of rabbits out there 'cause they'd sowed it to wheat.

We had a spotlight and a man standing up in the back of the pickup with a .22. If the rabbit ran, he'd shoot in front of him a foot or so and turn him back. Then he'd shoot in front of him again. If he ran straight away, he shot over the top of him and he'd stop. Then we'd drive up and pitch that net on the rabbit and we'd have to jump off and get on it or he'd run off with it.

That's the way we got 'em, and we had *seventy-three* of them things in my basement. Lord God . . . stink! The maddest wife! I was taking alfalfa hay down there to 'em and she was having to water 'em, and mad! Uncommonly mad.

They were running loose in that basement and when you walked down there, quite a bit happened. Two or three of them had babies and they'd jump on you when you went down there. Don't think them momma rabbits won't jump on you and whack you with their hind feet.

We took a roll of chicken wire, that little chicken wire, and put it around the inside of the roping arena, and in the catch pen we had little boxes covered with gunny sacks. We ran those rabbits the day before the roping. We turned them a-loose in the calf chute and busted their butts and made 'em run. When they found out there was a sanctuary on the other end, they'd go to it.

We ran 'em twice, and boy, that second time they made a bee line for that other end.

I don't remember how many ropers we had, but each one got two head of rabbits. A lot of them was local. Those old boys would nod for their rabbit and them old horses would come out of there hunting for a calf. The rabbit would stop and the horse would go on.

But there was one boy, I'd known him since he was little, his name was Clifton Smith. His daddy was Will T. Smith from Tell,

71

Texas, and he was a calf roper. Clifton later won the Cheyenne Frontiers Day calf roping.

He was smarter than the rest. He'd watched those other boys going after their rabbits. Nobody caught one and he figured out a plan.

He'd brought a little rope, wasn't as big around as a cigarette, and he didn't chase his rabbit. He just kind of headed it off. He didn't run out there and try to rope it like the others had done, 'cause you can't drag your slack on a jackrabbit.

He cut that rabbit off, and when it hit the fence and sat up, Clifton whapped a hoolihan on that general, got down, and brought him to us. And that's the only one that was caught out of them 73 rabbits. Clifton won all the money, all three places.

After the roping, we had to dispose of the rabbits. There were some greyhound people out there and we sold them the rabbits for six bits apiece. And when we paid the promotional expenses and took the price of the chicken wire off, I think I made $3.75 and lost two weeks' sleep.

After the rabbit roping, we kind of celebrated our fortunes and getting rich. We drank a little beer and I felt pretty bad the next morning. I just had a couple of days before I was supposed to go to work for the Miller Brothers. I had to get these horses taken care of. I'd already sent a bunch of them home but I had one mare left. She was tough but she was doing good.

She belonged to a farmer over at Kirkland. She was about eight or nine years old and had been in every bronc pen within five hundred miles of there. I was getting along real good with her. She was a half-Percheron and she weighted 1450. I started to get on her the next morning. She'd kick the fire out of you if you ever went for that stirrup. You was just fair game. So I turned the stirrup to get on her, but I thought, "Now, I've got to take her home tomorrow and that farmer ain't going to turn his stirrup around. He's going to step right back here and jump at it to get on this mare."

So I did it that way too, and that hussy kicked me and broke my leg!

I went to work for the Miller Brothers on crutches. I played my first job at Tinker Field, near Oklahoma City. I didn't use the crutches on the bandstand, just kind of kept my weight off of the leg. You can walk on your heel with a broke leg if you know how.

And then we went to Cheyenne, Wyoming. You ever been to Cheyenne? I don't know if it was the second or third day, but those crutches disappeared and I ain't seen 'em since.

One time while I was with Miller Brothers, we were playing in a skating rink somewhere in Arkansas, and we had three fiddles. There was an old boy in overalls come up there. I knew he was a fiddle player because he didn't pay much attention until the fiddles played.

When we took intermission, I went over to him and asked him if he played the fiddle. "Oh, not much," he said, and then I knew. If he'd said yes, I would have gone on. I asked if he'd play something with us and he said, "No, I'm sure not in you boys' class." I told him no, we were in a class to ourselves—a way by ourselves.

I invited him out to our bus and we talked about tunes, and when he found out I knew Eck Robertson, that broke the ice. He said, "Why don't you play some of Eck's music," and I said, "Because I can't. It's too hard. Can you play Eck Robertson's tunes?" He said he could.

I told the band leader that we ought to let that guy play. I gave him my fiddle and the band leader asked what key he wanted to play in, and the old boy said, "I don't know, it's right here." He didn't know the names of notes or chords.

And say, he played that "Sally Johnson" so well, it made water come into your eyes, sounded just like Eck Robertson playing it. And then we couldn't stop him. He just kept playing, and every chorus he played, it got a little bit better. Nobody really wanted to be the one to follow him.

If I hadn't encouraged him, we never would have heard him. Most bands wouldn't have taken the time, I'm sure. But there is so much talent in those hills! It's unreal. They'll play at home but they won't play for anyone. I don't even remember his name. That's sad.

Making Bob Wills's Band

In 1960 or '61 the Miller Brothers Band was playing at The Golden Nugget in Las Vegas, and I thought I saw Bob Wills out there in the audience. He had a little old snap-brim derby on. We played and did our thing reasonably well.

When the show was over, I went to the dressing room upstairs and he was in there. I'd already got crossways with some of them in the band and decided they weren't the group I was wanting to work with. As a matter of fact, I already had me a job lined up breaking horses for $125 a week.

And Bob said, "Say, I'm putting a new group together, and from what I heard, I sure would like to have you be a part of it."

I said, "Yes sir!"

I told him my schedule and he told me his, and we agreed to meet in Chickasha, Oklahoma, and that's the way it happened.

When I went to work for him, he said, "You're number 463." I asked him what he meant, did I have a cage number or what? He said, "No, you're the 463rd Texas Playboy."

Bob had a birthmark on the back of his neck but it didn't show up until he got mad about something. He always had a good haircut. He'd get a haircut twice a week, so the birthmark was never covered. When he walked to the microphone and we could see that birthmark, we knew that something had upset him. That was our sign to tread lightly: Don't play a wrong note, don't say a wrong word.

One time we were playing at the officers' club at the Amarillo Air Force base in, oh, '61 or '62. And Bob was having a good time, the band was sounding good and everybody was enjoying it. Then somebody come up there to talk to him.

Normally, he didn't talk to people. He'd send one of us down there to find out what they wanted. His back was hurting, you know, and he didn't feel like bending over, and if they had a song request, they would usually tell me or someone else.

But this old boy started up to the front and Bob spotted him. He could spot a spook at the back side of a dance hall, somebody who wasn't buying his music. He could spot 'em. And this old boy got about thirty feet from the bandstand and Bob said, "Sooey!" And I knew then that something was fixing to happen.

But he leaned down there and visited with him, then he backed up and said, "No, I'm sorry, we don't do that one. We don't know it."

I don't remember the song, but it was something that didn't fit our deal at all.

So the old boy went down to Tag Lambert, he was playing the guitar, and directly he come back. Bob leaned down there and the old boy said, "Tag told me that he could play it." When Bob stood up, that birthmark was *red.*

He said, "Maybe he can play it tomorrow night but he won't be doing it tonight because I told you we didn't know it. Forget it."

And he switched off that microphone and turned to Tag and said "I want to tell you something, little feller. If I tell one of these clowns that we don't know 'San Antonio Rose,' you had better forget that you know it."

When that birthmark got red, things began to tighten up and that band got to sounding quite a bit better.

Bob didn't get mad often, he really didn't. It took a lot to make him mad.

He told me one time, "Don't ever take a tip or have a kitty at a dance. If they put a quarter in there, they own you all night." I've seen people come up to the bandstand and put a ten dollar bill down, and he said, "No, you paid to hear that song when you came in the door."

Bob Wills was the most interesting man I ever met. He was the type of person who could make things happen. He believed in what he believed in. He didn't care if anybody else believed it, if he thought it would work, it came to pass.

One time I was worrying about my playing, didn't think I was playing good enough, which I wasn't, and I couldn't relax and really tie into it. And he knew that and he said, "Frankie, you're not playing a third of your potential. What's wrong?"

I said, "Bob, I just don't want to make a mistake."

He said, "Son, let me tell you something. Everything this band has done that was successful was a mistake in the beginning. When you play a bad note, it's gone. If it was wrong, try not to play it tomorrow night, but when you turn it loose, it's gone. When you find one you like, hang on to it. That's what I do."

And he would. He wouldn't play things the same way. If he got into a note that had the right sound to it and fit his mood, he'd hold on to her. He didn't worry about the meter.

One time the band was recording a song and one of the musicians quit playing. Bob asked him what was wrong.

"Bob, you're playing that song out of meter." Bob asked him what he meant by that. "Well, you're holding that note thirteen beats and you ought to be holding it just four." And he played it and showed Bob what he meant.

Bob said, "That's the way I feel it. That's the way I do it, whether it's right or wrong, and that's the way we're going to do it. If the Lord had written the first music, I wouldn't question you at all, but a man wrote the first music and for all you know, I may be smarter than he was. If you don't want to play it like this, put your fiddle up and be gone."

And the old boy left.

That's the way Bob was. He sure didn't mince any words with those recording people either. They'd try to get him to change something, and he'd say, "Now let me tell you something. We're going to play this song one more time. If you want it, you get it. If you don't want it, we won't even play it. We're gone."

And when he said it, that birthmark on the back of his neck would be bright red.

He was going to do things his way, and that's why he didn't do more movies. He didn't like those people in Hollywood telling his boys what to do. You didn't mistreat Bob Wills's people. You dealt with *him* and he'd deal with the band. But those Hollywood people don't do things that way. Whoever's handy, that's who they talk to, and Bob didn't like it.

One time he told me, "I swore if we ever got that movie contract fulfilled, we'd never do that again." But they'd talked him into signing another contract. He said, "I was on my way to sign a contract to do twelve more movies, and the closer I got the more I hated it."

He pulled over to a liquor store and they didn't find him for thirty days. That story ain't in any of the books, but that's what he told me.

In the beginning, when he was starting out, Bob's theory of being recognized was that bad publicity, *any* publicity, was better than none.

He said, "If it's bad, they'll remember it longer than the good. We might go into a cafe and them boys might run up and down the counter kicking people's plates off in their laps, but they'd sure remember it. They might leave a hotel with the water running on the top floor in the lavatory and I'd have to pay for it, but people remembered it."

Bob didn't get close to many people but some people were special to him. He was very reserved. He wasn't proud of his cotton pickin'. He was ashamed of it. He could just barely write his name and he was very conscious of that. He had a terrible inferiority complex. I don't know if he ever realized how much impact he had on the world. I wondered about that.

All of his boys were special to him. Some of them were there because he loved 'em and loved what they felt for him, and the others were there because he needed them.

He had an uncanny ability to read people and predict things. He told me six months before I quit that I was going to. He said, "Don't do it. It ain't worth it, what you're thinking about."

I said, "I don't know what you're talking about."

He said, "Yeah, you do. You're fixing to quit."

I said, "Bob, that's the farthest thing from my mind."

He said, "It might be right now, but it won't be. I know what I'm talking about. Don't do it. When the time comes that you're going to tell me you quit, don't tell me. I love you, I don't want you to leave me. I want you here."

About five months later, my wife called and said, "Son, these kids are going to have a daddy. If you want to be it, you'd better get your business gathered up and get to Texas."

I told Bob about it, and he said, "See there? What did I tell you?"

He could have been the world's greatest psychologist, to read people and help them. I learned a world of things about people from Bob Wills. He had the ability to look at a person and know what he would do in a crisis, if he'd flee and run or stay and help you.

Bob's secret was in his eyes. He could charm a rattlesnake with his eyes. They were going to do a movie about him and Betty Wills said, "I don't know who you'll get to play that part because I don't know anyone with eyes like Bob Wills."

He could do more with his eyes than anyone I ever knew. It was powerful. He could make you think that you were the greatest person in the world, or the sorriest, whichever he decided on, just by looking you in the eyes.

Bob had some of the crudest expressions you ever heard but everybody knew what he was talking about. He hired a drummer while I was with the band, a new drummer. I thought the kid was doing pretty good but he wasn't doing what Bob wanted.

He had us all in this rehearsal and he said to that drummer, "I don't know how to tell you this, but I want that rhythm section to sound like a freight train just about to run over you. You've got to have that *suction*, that whooooosh."

That was the way he would explain things.

When we were playing shows, Bob would get in a rut, playing the same tunes night after night. He'd get bored with what he was doing. He knew so many, many tunes but he didn't get a chance to play them. But every once in a while he'd think of one, or someone he'd known years ago would ask for one, and he'd play it.

These were songs he'd learned from his father and grandfather. They weren't sophisticated tunes, most of them, just old breakdown tunes. When one of them caught my fancy, I'd sure try to nail it down and learn it.

A lot of times, I was supposed to be playing with the band, but I'd lay out to see what he was doing on those things. It didn't go over well with him, but I was able to learn what I wanted to learn. Then, the first chance I got, I'd get him to show it to me.

While I was with the band, he didn't feel good a lot of the time. I know he didn't feel like doing it, but he did. He knew I was serious about learning those tunes.

We did quite a lot of this between shows at The Golden Nugget in Las Vegas. We'd play a forty-minute show and then another group would come on and play forty minutes, and while they played we would go to the dressing room and rest. That's when we'd do it, unless the dressing room was full of people, which a lot of times it was. I'd take his fiddle and mine into the dressing room and set them down. He'd see them and say, "Oh dear, not again!"

He was usually kind enough to show me what I wanted to know, but I knew when to ask and when not to. If he was mad at someone, you sure didn't want to bother him, and I tried not to catch him when he was feeling real bad. You could tell.

But that's how I learned most of those tunes. He'd put in little extra notes and change them around. That's what made Bob Wills's fiddle different from anyone else. I was aware of that and I wanted to learn it. A lot of those tunes were out of meter. When he found a note he liked, he'd hang on to it.

There was one in particular I remember. He said, "You don't need to fool with that one, son. You're not a good enough bow man to play it." It kind of hurt my feelings, but he was using some psychology on me. He knew I was going to learn that tune, and if he'd said anything else, I might not have.

He had one that I'm so sorry I didn't get, because he loved to play it. He called it "Scott Number 2." It had a little tail end on it and I put it on the end of my tune, "Between the Rivers." He taught me another one called "Stoney Point," and I've lost that one too. It was something like "Taters in the Sandy Land," had a G and E minor in it.

I never knew of Bob sitting down with anyone else and teaching him these old tunes. 'Course, I didn't know him until he was tired and not feeling good. He worked so hard on that band stand! Most of the time at dances, we wouldn't break for intermission. Sometimes he would hang his fiddle up and go to the bus and someone else would run the band for him. While I was with him, I called the tunes and set the tempo while he was off.

I'm so glad that he was a part of my life. He made my life so much more pleasant. I feel I was able to accomplish something that a lot of uneducated musicians couldn't have done.

Frankie McWhorter's first band at the first dance he ever played, Hedley, Texas, VFW, *circa* 1951. From left: Jesse Munsenbacher, Frankie McWhorter, Alvin Taylor, Billy Gusbell, Curtis Marchbanks, and Elton Murdock.

Touring U.S. military bases in Germany and Austria, *circa* 1953, with a thirty-three–person variety show. At an NCO club in Stuttgart. From left: Frankie McWhorter, (Corporal) Skeen, Duane Ellingson, and Coy Almond.

With Clyde Chesser and the Texas Village Boys, television show, Fort Worth, *circa* 1956. "We played nine TV shows a week—six in Waco, two in Tyler, and one in Fort Worth."

Clyde Chesser and the Texas Village Boys, *circa* 1956. Chesser had changed Frankie's name. "Leon Ralph" is Leon Rausch.

The Miller Brothers Band leaves for Puerto Rico, *circa* 1957. "We got in the eye of a hurricane and that damn thing fell, they said, six hundred feet. Broke the neck offa that Eck Robertson fiddle." Clockwise from left: Leon Gibbs, Curly Hollingsworth, Dutch Ingram, Frankie McWhorter, Paul Wayne, Jim McGraw, Bill Jordan, and (center) Bob Womack.

The Miller Brothers Band at the MB Corral, Wichita Falls, *circa* 1959. From left: Bill Jordan, Brent Kent, Bobby Rhodes, Dutch Ingram, Frankie McWhorter, Jim McGraw, Curly Hollingsworth, and Arden Bruce.

Bob Wills and the Texas Playboys at The Golden Nugget, Las Vegas, *circa* 1961. From left: Casey Dickens, Wade Peeler, Frankie McWhorter, Bob Wills, Gene "Tag" Lambert, Gene Crownover, and George Clayburn.

Cover of tour calendar provided by booking agency, 1962.

Page from Frankie McWhorter's tour calendar, 1962.

Bob Wills Day, Turkey, Texas, 1987. From left: Bobby Boatwright, Frankie McWhorter, and Joe Holley.

Bob Wills Day, 1987. From left: Tiny Moore, Bobby Boatwright, Frankie McWhorter, and Joe Holley. "You won't get any more of these [photos]."

86

Bob Wills Day, 1987. From left: Tiny Moore, Bobby Boatwright, and Frankie McWhorter.

Bob Wills Day, 1989. From left: Jimmy Young, Frankie McWhorter, Jack Bailey, Glenn "Blub" Rhees, Clarence Cagle, and Eldon Shamblin.

From left: Frankie McWhorter, Bob Wills, and Luke Wills, Denver, Colorado, 1961.

Bob Wills Stories

When the band was traveling on the bus, Bob wouldn't sleep but two hours a night. He'd just lay there listening to his radio. I've been with him when I thought he was asleep and they'd play a Bob Wills tune and he'd turn it off. He wouldn't listen to it.

He talked to me a lot at night. We'd be in that bus going down the road. He'd sit in that front seat with the radio going. We'd be in our beds. He'd say, "Frankie, you asleep?" And I never was asleep, I was always thinking about what a bad job I'd done and how to correct the bad notes I'd played. And he'd say, "Would you like to visit a little?"

He'd talk about the people he'd grown up with back in Hall County. I knew their kids who were my age. I knew a bunch of those people and he'd want to talk about them. And ho told me some funny stories, like the one about the feller who had a wooden leg.

He'd got his leg shot off some way. I knew the guy and knew his kids. He was a bootlegger back there in Hall County, and he had an artificial leg.

Bob asked me if I knew him, and I said, "Sure do. I've bought a little whiskey from him occasionally." And Bob said, "So have I! You know, he didn't have the money to buy himself a wooden leg so he whittled one out of a fencepost and fixed it below his knee where it was shot off.

"One afternoon several of us had been drinking that old homebrew and was going to Lakeview, and we all needed to relieve ourselves. Bad. We saw some dust down the road and we knew there was a car coming. We didn't want to just step out on the side of the road, you know, because it might have been a family in the car. So we stopped at this little rock bluff and went around behind it to do our business.

"Somebody said, 'There's a rattlesnake!' And somebody else said, 'There's another one!' They were all around us, already coiled up and mad, and we went to running over people to get back to that car. And here came this old bootlegger, hopping on his good leg, and there was a rattlesnake playing Yankee Doodle on his fencepost leg. And when he got away from the rattlesnakes, he fell down."

Bob told me another story. You know, back in the old days they used cisterns to store their water. Some of them had cement around the tops but some of them just had wooden sticks over the cistern.

Well, when Bob was a young man, he was playing at one of those old farm houses one night. Not unlike anybody else, Bob had an eye for a pretty girl, and he said there was the prettiest little thing come in there he'd ever seen, and with the biggest old boy.

He said, "I just kind of looked this deal over. It had been raining and I tuned that fiddle up to a B instead of A, and it sure did ring. If it's wet weather, you tune that thing up to a B and it'll reach a mile and a half."

I don't know why or how Bob knew that, but that's what he told me.

And he said he had that fiddle run up there, and there was another old boy playing with him. He waited until that girl's boyfriend went out to have a drink and then he went and got that girl.

He said, "She'd already looked me in the eye, and I eased her out the back door. I was out there talking to her and I noticed this cistern. I'd built forty of them. We made our arrangements to see one another later on and we went back in. Just as we went back in, her boyfriend come in and saw us. He had a bunch of people with him."

Bob had some kinfolks there and they all came running over to him and told him he'd better get out of there, that old boy was fixing to kill him.

So they went out the back door and started running around the house, and the others started chasing them.

Bob said, "I knew it was just a matter of time until one of them would think of going back the other way. So we come around to this cistern and I said to my kinfolks, 'Help me here just a minute.' We moved that cistern lid over about three feet and every one of them boys fell into the cistern."

He told me another story about breaking those bronc mules back in the twenties and early thirties. There was a lot of young mules around but nobody had any money to have them broke, and a lot of those farmers didn't know how or wouldn't take the time.

He said his daddy would take in six of those bronc mules for two of them. The farmer would take him six and come get four. And the way he'd start 'em off is, when he'd take a bale of cotton into Turkey, he had an old team that he'd pull the wagon with and he'd tie those bronc mules onto the side of the old mules.

They had to go across a place called the Ox Bow Bridge. It was more than a quarter-mile long, maybe three-eighths of a mile, and it wasn't wide enough for two-way traffic. And it had no rails on it. There were three places in it where it was quite a bit wider, where people could meet and pass one another. One could pull over and the other could go by.

And the old man told Bob, "Son, hook up them bronc mules when you take that load of cotton in. Before you get to that bridge, unhook 'em and put halters on 'em and tie 'em behind that wagon. It ain't wide enough for four mules."

And Bob said, "Yes sir."

Bob told me, "I did that two or three times, and one day I was going along and met an old cowboy named Perk Hancock."

Perk always had a good car and good whiskey. And he had a gallon of whiskey with him that day. I don't know whether he'd made it or somebody else had made it, but it was in a big jar.

Bob said, "Perk, why don't you go with me? Bring that whiskey and we'll take this load to the cotton gin."

Perk said all right and got in the wagon. Bob said the more whiskey they drank, the closer they got to the bridge and the more he didn't feel like he needed to unhook them mules. He thought, "They ain't going to fall off that bridge."

He said, "I got about fifty feet from that bridge and I went to frailing them old mules' butts. They switched their tails and away they went. Every once in a while, one of them bronc mules would stick a foot over the side but they weren't going to fall off of that bridge."

He said, "We got to the other side and I thought, why haven't I thought of this before?"

So on the last load of cotton, Poppa Wills said, "I believe I'll go with you and settle up with those folks." And Bob thought, "Uh oh, here we go." Poppa said, "Let's take a team of those bronc mules."

Bob told me, "I knew what was going to happen, and it happened just that way. We got about fifty feet from the bridge and Poppa said, 'Son, don't you think we ought to unhook those mules?' I took hold of those old mules' mouths and they switched their tails and away they went across that bridge."

Bob said, "We got to the other side and I knew he was going to stop them mules and whip me with the check lines. He didn't say anything for a good while, and then he said, 'Jim Bob, you know what I think? I think you haven't been unhooking those young mules.'"

Bob told me that the old man never said another word about it.

Bob loved horses. One time he bought seventy-seven mares from the RO ranch in Old Mexico. He had seven studs, eleven mares to the stud, and had them programmed. He studied the mare and the horse and chose the breeding on them.

And then he bought a horse from Bob Crosby. It was a gelding, a Thoroughbred racehorse named Reservation, and Bob paid fifteen thousand dollars for him. At that time, it was the most money ever paid for a horse.

Bob Crosby was a great cowboy and steer roper. He used to take old Reservation and pen three geese in a stovepipe, in the middle of an arena. Wills happened to be there one night and saw the horse work, and he bought him.

Bob told me, "I bought him for one reason. Them Hollywood fellers thought they were cowboys and the whole world thought they were cowboys. You can't believe how much fun I've had putting those son of a bucks on that horse!"

He called their names. People like Russell Hayden and Tex Ritter. They were noted "cowboys" throughout the world. Bob thought, "Wouldn't it be hilarious to see Tex Ritter scooting on his belly?"

He said, "There was an old crippled mare named Penny RO who'd be about twenty yards behind the others when they came into that corral. I'd send those Hollywood boys out to gather the mares, and when all of them were in but Penny, I'd jump out there and wave my hat and she'd turn back. And when she did, Reservation would lock himself in that ground and go get her."

He said, "Now, they could live through that, but when Reservation headed her and started *back* down the fence, those boys would go sailing off. They couldn't ride him."

He said, "I've had every supposed 'cowboy' implanted in that ground out there. I want to tell you something, son, when Reservation came back down that fence, you'd better have everything together."

Bob would tell me stories like that because he knew I was a horseman and could understand them. He couldn't tell other people because they wouldn't know what he was talking about.

Just like he told me, "We'd be plowing or cultivating, and we always worked them old bronc mules, two of them. I'd tell those black boys, 'I'm going to ride old Rosie to the house tonight.'

"'Oh Mister Bob, that mule buck you off.'

"'That mule can't buck me off. He don't even buck. He just runs around.'"

Bob said they didn't have any britching on the mules, just some old trace chains, and Bob would run one of those chains under the mule's front legs and hook it to the hames. Every time he'd start to buck, Bob would jerk the chain and scare him. It would hit him under the leg and he'd start running around but wouldn't buck, and Bob could ride him to the house.

93

So the next day Bob would say, "Say, Ezra, I rode old Rosie yesterday. Why don't you ride her?"

"Mister Bob, I don't know."

"Well, I guess you're scared."

"Naw sir, I ain't scared."

Then Ezra would get on that mule and it would buck him off. Bob had an understanding about everything, including horses. He absolutely loved horses. I never saw him ride a horse so I can't say if he was a good horseman, but he was good at everything else he did, so maybe he was.

He had his deal set up near Fresno, California, where he kept all them RO mares and had big orchards but he couldn't make any money with it. At that time he was also building that Bob Wills Ranchhouse in Dallas and had all these construction people hired.

He had that ranch and that's where he was going to settle down. He would have played the Bob Wills Ranchhouse twice a month and let somebody else handle it the rest of the time, Eldon or Johnny Gimble.

Bob told me, "One morning I was in Dallas and a fellow called me and said, 'Are you Bob Wills?' And I said yes sir. He said, 'I'll see you in your office in thirty minutes.'"

Bob said, "I kind of doubt that because I wasn't planning to go to my office. The man said, 'You'd better plan on it. I'm with the IRS and you owe us seventy-eight thousand dollars and we don't think you've got it.'"

Bob said, "You're right. I ain't got it but I'll be there in thirty minutes and we'll talk about it."

He said it scared him to death. He had to sell that ranch in Fresno and that Bob Wills Ranchhouse in Dallas. They gave him seventy-two hours to come up with seventy-eight thousand dollars or they were going to send him up. He told me that either place was worth more than that. The exact same thing happened to Blackie Crawford. He was a band leader who had the Western Cherokees. He started Ray Price, gave him his first job. He started George Jones, started Lefty Frizzell. He was a man who knew talent. But the same thing happened to him, trouble with the IRS, and they locked him up in Longview, Texas. They put him in jail.

He and Bob had some of the same advisors, and Bob thought there was something funny going on. Two sets of books, payments that weren't being sent to the right places.

Bob told me about buying this silver-mounted saddle. He ordered it from Garcia in Los Angeles. They had played a radio show and was fixing to leave and go to a dance when Garcia called and said the saddle was ready.

They were going within eight or ten blocks of this saddle company so he said, "Boys, let's just go by there and pick up my saddle." He told me, "If we hadn't had a ten-piece band, we never would have been able to load that thing. That son of a gun weighed more than a bale of cotton!"

Bob told me about the time he called up Irving Berlin and ate him out for changing the words to "San Antonio Rose." Berlin had published the song on sheet music.

Bob said, "I never could get out by the time it was popular. I had to stay in the room all the time and couldn't go anywhere had to have my meals sent to me and bodyguards when I'd go to play.

"One night the boys in the band came to me and said they'd heard four different bands playing 'San Antonio Rose.' They'd all played it the same way, and it was wrong.

"I said, 'What's the matter with it?' They didn't know. I said, 'Tomorrow, go buy some sheet music and play it and find out.'"

Bob had one man in the band who could read music, and he'd read it and teach the others. He found out that Irving Berlin had changed the melody on 'San Antonio Rose.' He told Bob what it was. Bob told me this story himself.

He said, "I was pretty upset about it and I got on that phone. Irving's secretary answered the phone, and I said, 'Is Irving Berlin there?' She said, 'Yes sir, but he's in a meeting right now.' And I said, 'Get the SOB on the phone, I want to talk to him.' She said, 'Who is this?' I said, 'Bob Wills.' She said, 'Just a minute.'

"Then Irving got on the phone and I said, 'Irving, why did you change my song?'

"And he said, 'Bob, we just felt that the melody needed to be more dominant.'

"And I said, 'I'm sending you another sheet of it, and if a fly specks on it between now and the time you get it, it had better be on that sheet music.'"

Irving Berlin had to pull all the old music and put in the new version. That was the "New San Antonio Rose."

The Drinking Problem

There was something in Bob's background that triggered his drinking. He had started out as a poor person. He could associate and mingle with any kind of people, but basically Bob was still a poor boy. When he got depressed or had too much on his mind or got tired, which he had to have been because everyone else was, he'd revert back to his childhood days and go to drinking.

People he'd known years and years ago, those were the ones who could get him to take a drink. The other ones couldn't. He wouldn't drink with a rich person. But he'd sure drink with a poor boy because he still considered himself a—how did he put it? "A lucky poor boy," that's the way he said it.

There was a little guy in Amarillo who'd get him drunk. Every time we'd go through Amarillo, this little whelp would give him whiskey. It made me mad, because when Bob got to drinking, he'd be drunk for two weeks. We just had to do without him and take all this abuse from the club owners and the public. And at that particular time, I was fronting his band when he wasn't there.

And say, they came down on me! "Where is Bob? Where's old Bob?"

Well, I'd say that Bob was under a doctor's care, not feeling well. I had a statement that I wrote out myself and signed Dr. So-and-so.

But this one little old guy, he got on that bus in Amarillo one night. We were going to Clovis to play at the Purple Onion. It sounds like a hippie joint but it wasn't. It belonged to some bulldogger, can't remember his name.

Well, on the way over there, Bob was sitting up front—asleep, I thought. This little guy sat down right behind Bob and I went up and sat down beside him. I grabbed him by the arm and whapped him in the ribs pretty good with my elbow.

I said, "Now, I'm telling you. You'd better quit giving him whiskey. Bob's been straight and then you mess things up. It isn't good for him. I love him."

He said, "So do I."

And I said, "Then why do you give him that whiskey?"

Then Bob raised up. "By God, he gives me that whiskey because I ask him to, and don't say anything else to him."

The fellow went with us to Clovis and I caught him outside. I said, "Let me tell you something, hoss. If you ever bring Bob Wills another drink of whiskey, I am personally going to beat you to death. And if you don't think I can do it, let's try it right now."

Bob Wills could get a drink of whiskey in the Methodist Church in Higgins, Texas, if he wanted it. I'll bet a thousand dollars he could. You couldn't stop him.

One Saturday night we'd played in Las Vegas and were going to Hollywood to record on Monday. We had a practice session on Sunday. Bob hadn't made a show in Las Vegas. Two weeks we'd been there without him. I'd run the band and then I'd have to go stay with him. He didn't want anybody else around him for some reason.

I'd been through this for two weeks and my nerves were absolutely shattered. I was give out just from the shows alone. We'd been doing eight forty-minute shows a night.

About four o'clock in the morning, we were traveling in the bus, and he said, "Frankie, come here." I went up there and he said, "Frankie, I need another drink." I told him I didn't have any. He said, "I know that but I need a drink."

I said, "But this is Sunday morning. We can't get a drink." We wanted him straight for that practice session, see.

He hollered at that bus driver, "Pull over here at this motel." Then he gave me a twenty-dollar bill and said, "You go in there and tell whoever's running it that you need some whiskey for Bob Wills."

I said, "Bob, whoever's in there will scalp me for waking him up at this time of the morning and asking for whiskey."

He said, "Tell 'em it's for me."

I said, "All right." So I went in there and rang the bell. Directly here came this old boy with hair down in his eyes. He said, "What do you want? We're full and we've got our no-vacancy sign on."

I said, "Yes sir, I know that but . . . I need a drink of whiskey."

He said, "I ought to kill you for getting me up!" Which I knew he'd say. My reaction would have been the same at four o'clock in the morning. He said, "This is not a liquor store. This is a motel."

I said, "Look, Bob Wills sent me in here to ask."

"Bob!" he said. "Where's old Bob?"

"He's out there in that bus."

He went over there and looked and said, "By golly! Let me check." He went back there and checked and said, "I ain't got a drop of whiskey, but I've got this."

That was the first time I'd ever seen one of those big cans of Colt .45 malt liquor.

He said, "You take this to him. We had a party here tonight and it hasn't been too long since it was opened. This is all I've got, and apologize to Bob for me."

I knew by his reaction that he wouldn't take that twenty-dollar bill, so I just slipped it under something on the counter. I told Bob, "He wouldn't take that money but I kind of left it with him."

He said, "That's good!" And he drank that and went to sleep.

That's the way he was. He could get a drink when he wanted one. After that recording session, we were staying in the Hollywood Colonial Motel. It was a shiny deal.

I'd already taken nine hundred dollars away from one of the maids. She was coming out of his room and I just happened to be coming in, and she had a roll of money in her hands. I said, "Where'd you get that?"

She said, "Mr. Bob gave it to me." I got it. Nine hundred dollars she had! I counted it. See, I was supposed to take him from there to Bowie, Arizona, and from there I had to take him to Tulsa. We never made it to Bowie and his wife called, mad as heck, thought we weren't doing our job, taking care of him.

But anyway, I had a talk with all those porters and bellboys. I told them, "Let me tell you something. If Bob Wills gets a drink of whiskey, you're out of a job, and maybe dead on top of that."

And they said, "No sir, we won't do that. We love Mr. Bob, we ain't going to give him anything. He's sick."

Of course, that's when he wanted it the most, when he was "sick."

We had to catch a plane at 11:30 that morning to go to Tulsa. I went in the room and Bob said, "I feel bad. I need a drink."

I said, "I know exactly what you need, Bob. How does some V-8 Juice sound to you?"

He said, "Frankie, that sounds better than whiskey. Would you go get me some?" So he reached for his money and didn't have any. He said, "You got any money?"

I said, "Yes sir, I've got a little bit."

He said, "You got enough? I don't know what happened to my money."

I said, "I've got a little bit of money. I'll be back in five minutes."

The store was just at the other end of the block. I went down there and bought two of those big cans of V-8 Juice. He wouldn't drink those little cans. He drank out of the big ones, and he could drink two of them, just like that.

I got two big cans and went back, and when I went into that room he was sitting on the bed with his hat and his boots and shorts on. He had a fifth of whiskey and he'd already drunk half of it.

I got it away from him and poured it in the commode, and he got mad about that. He fired me. I said, "Well, that's fine. If you don't want me, that's fine, Bob."

He said, "You ain't got any respect for whiskey. Anybody who'd pour out good whiskey ought to be killed!"

I said, "Under most circumstances, I'd have to agree with you, but under this one I can't."

This was like 8:30 in the morning, so I ordered a pot of coffee and got him straight. We got in a cab going to the airport, and we'd been riding in that cab for almost an hour and a half. I was up in the front with the driver, and I smelled whiskey.

Bob was in the back with some lady. I don't know who she was, someone going to the airport, I guess. I smelled this whiskey and turned around, and he had a pint of it turned up.

I got it away from him, and he slapped the fire out of me!

I said, "Where'd you get that?"

And he said, "That ain't important. The important thing is that I've got it—or had it."

Well, by the time we got to the airport, he was drunk and they wouldn't let him on the plane. So we had to go back, rerent the rooms, reschedule our flight, call Mrs. Wills: "We've missed our plane. I don't know when we'll be in Tulsa but I'll call you from Dallas or wherever I can."

So I got him another flight scheduled about ten o'clock that night. I said, "You take another drink of whiskey, Bob, and me and you are falling out."

He said, "Well, I won't, I promise. I feel bad and I won't."

So he didn't. We got in the air, and we hadn't been in the air five minutes when those stewardesses came around. He said, "Honey, come here!" And here came three or four of them, they just swarmed him with those little bottles. By the time we got to Tulsa, he was wiped out. I was having to hold him up to get him off the plane.

He said, "Where are we at?" I told him Tulsa, Oklahoma. He said, "Tulsa! What are we doing in Tulsa?"

I said, "Well, there's a pretty lady waiting on you here."

"A pretty lady? Are you talking about Betty? Have you got Betty here?"

I said, "She's right there."

And about that time she came over, and he straightened up and went to walking just as straight as a sober man. She was the only person in the world that he was afraid of, and she wasn't any bigger than a minute.

101

Here's a funny story Bob told me. The band had been playing at some club in California. The bus was broke down and they were hauling the instruments in a U-Haul trailer—had it on the back of a car—and traveling in two or three station wagons.

They finished playing on Saturday night and didn't have to play again until the next Wednesday.

Bob told me, "I got to drinking a little bit, more than I realized, I guess, because that band vanished."

Which they did. He'd get to drinking and they'd just disappear—except one. Someone had to take care of him. The last one to leave got that job.

Bob said, "Kelso and somebody else, I don't remember who it was, had planned a fishing trip and had reservations at some motel up in the mountains. For two nights. And when they come by there and saw me, they just stuck me in that trailer and went on."

He said, "After a while, my tongue was stuck to the roof of my mouth and it was thick. It was hot back there, I couldn't breathe, I was sick and throwing up and it was stinking in there. And I thought of every way I could kill them son of a bucks without getting caught. I thought of several ways.

"I knew they had to stop for gas before long because we'd been driving for a long time. And pretty soon they stopped. I went to beating on that trailer.

"The filling station attendant said, 'Somebody's in that trailer, did you know that?'

"And one of the boys said, 'Yeah, we're working for the California Insane Asylum and we're transporting a patient. He thinks he's Bob Wills.'"

Bob said, "I beat on that trailer and that old kid wouldn't answer. I knew the boys had gone to the restroom. I said, 'I'm Bob Wills! Let me out of here, I need to talk to you.' But that old kid never said a word.

"Directly, the boys come back out and the attendant said, 'You know, that son of a gun *is* crazy. He does think he's Bob Wills!'"

Bob said, "When we got to the top of that mountain and they opened that trailer door, I was so glad to see them, I just hugged their necks."

One time we were playing a job at night. Bob had been drinking and I didn't think he could play. He was asleep when we got there so I locked the door of the bus from the outside so nobody could get in—and he couldn't get out. We didn't want him coming in there. Well, that sure didn't set well with him and he told me this story.

It was in February. The band had been playing in Lawton, Oklahoma, on a Friday night and they were playing in Amarillo on Saturday.

Bob had gotten into his cups a little bit, and on the way to Amarillo they'd made several stops and got some whiskey.

He said, "When we got to Amarillo, they thought I was a little too tight to be in there, so they locked me in that bus. But I was quite a bit more sober than some of them SOBs in there playing with the band and I was listening to them in the bus. About midnight, a blizzard blowed in and snow and ice covered the windshield of that bus. I was freezing to death in there.

"When they played that last tune, I took the fire extinguisher and broke out both windshields. They come out there and said, 'What happened to this bus?' I told them, 'I was about to suffocate and couldn't breathe, so I just broke 'em out, you smart son of a bucks. You do know that we're playing in Albuquerque at three o'clock tomorrow afternoon, don't you?'

"They said, 'We can't drive without a windshield.' And I said, 'We'll either be there or we'll be somewhere between here and there.'"

Bob said, "I had a twelve-piece band. One man would drive a few miles into that blizzard and then he'd freeze out. The whole front end of the bus was full of ice and snow, and I'd tell 'em, 'Change drivers.' It took the whole band to drive us to Albuquerque."

After he'd told me that story, he looked at me and said, "You know, I was never locked in that bus again until tonight."

And I never locked him in there again.

"San Antonio Rose" and Afterthoughts

I've heard a lot of stories about how "San Antonio Rose" came about. Here's what Bob told me.

He was working as a barber in Roy, New Mexico, and one day a little Mexican fellow came in. Bob had his fiddle laying there and the man saw it. Bob couldn't understand Spanish and the other guy couldn't understand English, but he gestured and asked Bob if he played. Bob didn't want to, so he said no. So the man asked if he could play Bob's fiddle, and Bob said he could.

Bob said, "He played 'The Spanish Two-Step' and I locked the door where he couldn't get out and nobody else could get in, and I made him stay there until he taught me that and 'Maiden's Prayer.' Finally he nodded. I didn't know whether he needed to go to the bathroom or if I was doing it right, but I let him out."

That Mexican taught him those two tunes.

Later on, he recorded "The Spanish Two-Step" and it was a big hit for him, the biggest thing going at that time. It was a number one record all over the country.

Well, years later he was recording for Columbia and the old gentleman who was in charge of it was named Uncle Art Satherley. The band was going to record for three days in Dallas.

Satherly said, "Bob, we need another tune like that 'Spanish Two-Step.'"

Bob said, "Don't worry about it, we have one."

They recorded for three days and everybody was just numb. The boys had put their instruments up, and here came the Colonel out and said, "Where is my 'Spanish Two-Step' song, Bob?"

"I just completely forgot about it," Bob said. "Boys, let's break out your instruments again and do this song."

The Colonel went back in the control room and the boys asked Bob what they were going to do. Bob said, "I don't have any idea. I'm going to play the bridge of 'The Spanish Two-Step' backwards, and Leon, when I get through, you do anything you want to do and let's get the heck out of here."

They played it through for time and the Colonel came running out of there with his eyes wide open, said, "Bob, what do you call tune?"

Bob said, "You know, we haven't named it. We were going to let you name it. This tune's especially for you and you can name it anything you want to."

He said, "I'm going to call it 'San Antonio Rose.'"

"You call it anything you want to. We're tired and we're getting out of here."

Bob told me, "If that little old Mexican hadn't come in there to get a haircut, not near as many people would have known who Bob Wills was."

That's the story he told me, and he told me this when we were talking about the mistakes I was making in the band. He said, "Now, 'San Antonio Rose' is one instance of a mistake. We just did it! Nobody knew what we were doing. We just did something to get out of there."

When I was with the band, Bob was very dissatisfied with where he was. He knew he'd been a success. He'd had the greatest musicians in the world working for him, ten or twelve of them at a time, and when I was working for him, we only had seven. I know Bob had to feel that he was going downhill. He wasn't, but he felt like it.

I think Bob knew what he was doing. He was creating a music all its own. He was proud of it and he sure didn't want anyone making light of it.

Some people—let's say musical people with years of studying—didn't respect him as a musician. He'd play out of tune on occasion and he'd break meter quite often. The people who were studied and professional knew that they were right and he was wrong. But what they didn't take into consideration was that *he was Bob Wills*, and he was signing the checks.

Bob would never say a bad word about any type of music. He might not say anything, but he wouldn't criticize songs he heard on the radio, because he figured anything on the radio was a success, and he wouldn't criticize success. He played that radio all the time. He'd say, "Boys, I heard Patsy Cline doing a song on the radio. I don't remember the name but it was something about 'Crazy.' Get it. It's going to be a hit." Then he heard Bobby Vinton doing "Roses Are Red." Nobody in the band had heard it but Bob heard it, and he said, "Say, this is going to be a smash and we need to be a-doing it before it is."

That's the way he wanted to do things and he never was wrong. He never told us to learn a tune that didn't become a number one tune within six weeks or two months.

Bob Wills had a funky blues sound. It was jazz, in a sense. He'd play a trombone note or a clarinet note on the fiddle, is what he was doing. He was feeling jazz. He was not a jazz musician but he always surrounded himself with them, and he sure knew who could do it and who couldn't.

He knew he wasn't the greatest fiddle player in the world and he had an inferiority complex about it. Bob couldn't play "Orange Blossom Special," there's no way he could, but *he didn't have to.* I had to, but he didn't.

Bob was the best man with a bow that I was ever associated with. Maybe some of the classical violinists were better, but for what he did, he was the best I ever saw. There's no way to explain it. He just was. He never would show me that. I mentioned it to him and he said, "That's just something you acquire over the years." He'd be playing a note real soft, and then it would be loud, then soft again—just however his mood was. And he never got a scratch out of his bow, when he was right and at himself. If he'd been partying a little bit, he might make a squeak occasionally, but if he was at himself, he never got a bad bow sound.

He played a tune one night that I'd never heard him play. It was really a bow tune. I said, "It sounded like you were pulling those notes out of there with a corkscrew."

106

On some of Bob's tunes, I have trouble with my bow, but I've got a friend down at Childress who's a heck of a bow man. He's been helping me, and I can see now some of the things Bob was doing that I didn't see, they happened so fast.

On those old breakdown tunes, if he wanted to emphasize a note, he'd hit it with an up bow. I always did it going down, but you can't put as much emphasis on it with a down bow, I don't know why. When he was playing with other fiddles, he'd just pull that old smooth bow. If he wanted to emphasize a note, he'd just roll his bow with his finger and make it louder.

Bob Wills played what he played, he played what he felt, and he played it in his own way. His feel for music and his determination to present his music the way he wanted it done has had a tremendous impact on the country-western field. They'll never get away from it.

Afterword

When a writer is asked to write an afterword, the result should be just that—an afterword. In this case I want to add a little to the story you have just read, to tell you a little more about Frankie McWhorter, and, in so doing, to talk about some of my other favorite people, Bob Wills and John Erickson.

Frankie McWhorter was born in Memphis, Texas, not more than twenty miles from the ranch where young Jim Bob Wills was living when he played the fiddle at his first dance. Frankie grew up in the same cowboy-ranch environment that Wills did. In his formative years, McWhorter listened to Bob Wills recordings, became a Wills fan, and, like Bob, began playing a fiddle while he lived on a ranch in West Texas. While he was cowboying on the famous JA Ranch, founded by Charles Goodnight, Frankie began learning the fiddle. An older cowboy on the JA "would whistle a tune, and I would play it." It was appropriate that he would learn to play fiddle on a cattle ranch in the West, because cowboys, ranch folk, and people in general in the western part of the United States have always been the most ardent fans of western swing, the style he played later in the Wills band. One reason Bob Wills's music was called western swing was to distinguish it from the more traditional swing music of the big bands on the East and West Coasts. Other reasons were its popularity in the West, the cowboy image reflected in the dress of Wills's Texas Playboys, and the western movies in which the band was featured.

There is much more to Frankie McWhorter than simply a cowboy image, more than a large hat, Levi's, big belt buckle, and cowboy boots. To many musicians, all these things are costume, image, and facade. Frankie is the real thing, a "cowboy" in the strictest sense of the word. He makes his living running a cattle ranch in the Panhandle of Texas, near the village of Higgins. He has a remuda of good "cow horses" and always has some colts and fillies he "breaks" (trains) for working cattle on the range.

At times he is a bronc buster—not by choice but by necessity. He told me about a young horse he was riding recently that decided to buck. He said, "Doc, he was the buckingest thing I've ever been on. He bucked so high that I looked down and one of those big ole water troughs looked about the size of a dime."

Frankie is what many of our historians of American folk music call a "cowboy fiddler." One of the many things Bob Wills and Frankie had in common was both were fiddlers and cowboys. It is not widely known, but Bob was a good cowboy and horseman. Throughout the history of their West Texas, cowboying and fiddling have usually gone together.

In 1960, Frankie McWhorter got his break in western music. Bob Wills gave him a job "playing fiddle alongside the master with the Texas Playboys." On the bandstand, he learned a great deal playing beside Bob Wills. Off the bandstand, Frankie would ask Bob how he played certain selections and about fiddle techniques. In his humble way, Bob would say, "You don't want to learn those little two-fingered deals." Frankie would answer, "Yes, I do," and Wills would take time to teach him.

Frankie never forgot some of the really old-time fiddle tunes Bob taught him, and in 1987 made an album called *Fiddle Tunes Bob Wills Taught Me.* The producer of "Panhandle Pilgrimage," an elaborate slide show of Amarillo history, asked Frankie to include one of those rare Bob Wills fiddle tunes as part of the background for the production. The producer from Cambridge, Massachusetts, himself a fan of Wills's music, told me, "It was one of the most beautiful, authentic, and moving things I've ever heard." All of us will be in McWhorter's debt for preserving this rare Bob Wills music that would otherwise have been lost to posterity. In the preceding pages, Frankie tells the reader about some of this music.

On the bandstand, Frankie learned to play the Bob Wills fiddle style. Off the bandstand, he learned a great deal about Wills's personality. As he discusses in this book, he observed

Wills at various times when he had bouts with the bottle. Frankie has emphasized this problem because he never could understand it and because he saw it hurt the man he idolized.

For an in-depth study of this aspect of Wills's life, the reader should consult my biography, *San Antonio Rose: The Life and Music of Bob Wills* (Urbana: University of Illinois Press, 1976), where I discuss this problem within the context of his entire life, and where I conclude that it was never the problem fans and those close to him thought it to be. Wills's drinking was periodic, never regular or continual; he would go six weeks, six months, a year, and, at one time three years without a drink. A musician who was in his band for years put it in proper perspective: "For a man who was supposed to drink a lot," he said, "Bob Wills drank less than anyone I know."

Frankie McWhorter is one of many former Texas Playboys who appreciated Bob Wills the man as much or more than Bob Wills the musician. There was something about the appeal of Wills's musical style that remains a mystery. His personal appeal to those who were fortunate enough to be close to him also remains an enigma. Frankie and many other of Wills's band members have told me that they do not know why, but they played better for Wills than for any other bandleader. "He made us play over our heads"—better than they could at any other time in their careers.

Despite Bob's drinking or any other character flaws he may have possessed, he had certain qualities, such as honesty, integrity, human compassion manifested in liberality and a philanthropic spirit, and an overall philosophy of life that "made us better men," Frankie remarked.

Frankie and I have discussed Bob Wills for hours at a time, Frankie from his own experience and I speaking for the dozens I have interviewed. On one occasion, Frankie said, "When I had personal problems, whether it was a marital problem, a drinking problem, or if I had not been doing what I should, I would go to Bob." Wills, he said, "had a way of talking about something else and at the same time telling you to get your life straightened out without speaking directly on your problem or preaching to you.

111

He always gave me good advice and would help me with my problems."

McWhorter concluded, "He never ever told me anything wrong about how to live life. Boy, I miss him. I've needed him so many times since he died. He was my counselor, my psychologist, my dearest friend when I needed him." I do not think Frankie, in the text that precedes this, felt he could express these feelings without appearing too sentimental and emotional.

To borrow the words of a Broadway song, I have written about two of "my favorite things"—Frankie McWhorter and Bob Wills. Now, I want to conclude by at least mentioning the writer whose idea it was for Frankie to tell his story. It seems trite, but John Erickson really "needs no introduction." He is one of our best known and admired writers and storytellers in Texas and the West. I have long admired John Erickson's work but had never met him until he approached me regarding this afterword. His writings are unique, and his style is original, distinctive, and refreshingly free. He has that rare ability to write in such a way as to appeal to everyone from a little child to a mature adult. He has made Hank the Cowdog into a western hero, whose antics are appealing, interesting, and enlightening. John has let Hank tell the story of the life of the plain people that Erickson has studied for so long.

John has written on a variety of areas of western life and has helped to preserve the history and cultural heritage of the life and the people he admires. Other writers have written on the same subjects. What is different and so important about Erickson's work is that *people read it*. John Erickson and Frankie have written about western life and culture in the preceding pages. But this will not be the last we will hear of Frankie McWhorter and John Erickson. Other volumes will follow that will tell us more about Frankie the fiddler and the cowboy.

Charles R. Townsend